Developing Early
Maths Skills Outdoors

Activity ideas and best practice for teaching and learning outside

by Marianne Sargent

Dedication

This book is for my Dad.

Thank you for everything you have done for me.

Acknowledgements

Thanks must go to Peter Lambert, Vicki Cawthorn and the children at Chinley Primary School, High Peak, Derbyshire for inviting me in to the reception class to join in with their outdoor activities and allowing the use of a number of photographs.

Published by Practical Pre-School Books, A Division of MA Education Ltd, St Jude's Church, Dulwich Road, Herne Hill, London, SE24 0PB.

Tel: 020 7738 5454 www.practicalpreschoolbooks.com

Associate Publisher: Angela Morano Shaw

© MA Education Ltd 2015

Design: Alison Coombes fonthillcreative 01722 717043

All images © MA Education Ltd. All photos taken by Lucie Carlier, with the exception of the following: p.17 © iStockphoto.com/PureDynamics; p.14 (bottom left), p.29 (top right), p.37, p.38, p.46, p.49, p.58, p.62, p.66 (top left) p.70 (bottom right) and p.73 (top right) taken by Marianne Sargent.

ISBN 978-1-909280-83-0

Developing Early
Maths Skills Outdoors

by Marianne Sargent

Contents

Introduction

About the series

This series is intended for early years students and practitioners working with children aged two to five years. It aims to demonstrate how outdoor provision is just as important as the indoor classroom and to highlight the wealth of opportunities the outdoor environment provides for teaching basic skills and concepts in maths, science and literacy.

In her review of the Early Years Foundation Stage (EYFS) in England, Dame Tickell (2011) recommended a focus on 'how children learn rather than what they learn'. She identified three characteristics of effective learning; playing and exploring, active learning and creating and thinking critically. The books in this series outline the basic concepts and skills that underpin maths, science and literacy and show how the outdoor environment promotes an active, social and exploratory pedagogical approach to early learning.

Dame Tickell also singled out three 'prime' areas of learning; communication and language, personal, social and emotional development, and physical development. She identified these as fundamentally important for laying secure foundations in preparation for more formal education.

Therefore, these books promote early years practice that:

● Involves active practical activities that prompt lively debate and conversation, enabling children to develop the communication and language skills they need to find out about the world and make sense of new information, as well as discuss, extend and evaluate ideas;

- Gives children the chance to practise large and fine motor control, which is not only essential for cognitive development, but important in terms of gaining the strength and co-ordination needed for future writing and recording;

- Fosters physical and playful activity, promoting healthy personal, social and emotional development by reducing stress, improving mood and boosting motivation and learning.

The books contain a wealth of ideas for enhancing continuous outdoor provision, as well as planning focussed maths, science and literacy activities that exploit the unique qualities of the outdoor environment. They also provide advice on planning and assessment, where to find resources and recommendations for further reading. Throughout each book there are links to all four British early years curricula.

Developing Maths Outdoors

It is through active social early years experiences that children eventually become capable of logical, creative and critical thought. The outdoor environment facilitates active and physical exploration of the world, where children learn and use language to make sense of what they encounter. They do this in an unrestricted space that allows for vocal discussion and argument, which extends their knowledge and helps them to form new thinking and ideas.

Early years pioneers Jerome Bruner (1966) and Jean Piaget (1952) advocate physical exploration that helps children to develop understanding of basic concepts. They believe children internalise the knowledge they gain through hands-on experience and this later leads to more complex abstract thought. This theory is supported by the hugely influential Researching Effective Pedagogy in the Early Years (REPEY) and Effective Provision of Pre-school Education (EPPE) research projects, which advocate planning practical experiences for children to 'actively construct conceptual knowledge' (Siraj-Blatchford et al., 2002) through a balance of taught and 'freely chosen yet potentially instructive child-initiated activities' (Siraj-Blatchford et al., 2004).

Children develop mathematical sense by trying things out and playing with ideas. The outdoor environment is the ideal arena for planning maths activities that would otherwise be impractical, unattractive or impossible indoors. When outside children develop a sense of number by talking together, collecting natural objects and playing games; they explore size, shape and space while building on a large scale and tackling physical challenges; and they learn about capacity by digging holes in sand pits and filling buckets with water from hoses.

Lev Vygotsky (1986) further highlights the role of social interaction in learning. It is his contention that children extend and develop their thinking through discussion with more

knowledgeable others. This is again supported by the REPEY and EPPE research, which identify the need for good quality verbal interactions that extend and develop thinking. All four British early years curricula place much emphasis on the importance of mathematical conversation, introducing key vocabulary and teaching children the language they need to talk and think about their developing mathematical ideas.

When outside children are less restricted and have the freedom to sing, talk and shout, making it possible to engage in lively play, conversation and debate. Outside children have the space to recite and act out counting rhymes; they encounter large-scale mathematical problems, for example how many spades they need so everyone can help dig a large hole; they discuss and test mathematical ideas, such as how tall to build a ramp so that a toy car travels a certain distance; and they extend each others' learning by challenging one another's ideas, for instance when keeping score during team games.

The outdoor environment promotes active social learning, which is essential for acquiring early maths skills and developing an understanding of mathematical concepts. It is the ideal arena for children to voice their opinions, discuss problems, verbalise thoughts, argue with each other, test their theories against others and develop ever more accurate ideas. There is no need to be quiet outside in the open, where noise is carried away on the breeze.

Laying the Foundations for a successful future

The Effective Pre-school, Primary and Secondary Education (EPPSE 3-16) project report outlines how crucial the REPEY and EPPE research findings are. The report summarises the findings of the entire longitudinal study, which followed nearly 2,600 children from their early years through to the age of 16 and aimed 'to explore the most important influences on developmental pathways that lead to GCSE achievement, mental well-being, social behaviours and aspirations for the future'.

EPPSE reports that children who attended pre-school achieved 'higher total GCSE scores and higher grades in GCSE English and maths'. What's more, attending a high quality setting, where children are exposed to active, social learning experiences, was most beneficial and 'significantly predicted total GCSE scores as well as English and maths grades'. This was also a determining factor in terms of following an academic route into A levels, showing 'that the benefits of pre-school in shaping long term outcomes remain across all phases of schooling and last into young adulthood' (Sylva et al., 2014).

A well resourced outdoor learning environment is just as conducive to maths teaching as the indoor classroom.

The great outdoors

Outdoor provision is a fundamental aspect of early years education and is a statutory requirement across all four early years curricula. The EYFS (DfE, 2014) states that practitioners should provide flexible indoor and outdoor spaces where children can access stimulating resources that promote active exploration and play, while all the time being supported by knowledgeable adults who encourage them to think and ask questions.

The Scottish Curriculum for Excellence (SCE) promotes the outdoors as 'significant' to learning in literacy, numeracy and health and wellbeing, crediting it with helping young children 'make connections experientially, leading to deeper understanding within and between curriculum areas' (LTS, 2010).

The Welsh Foundation Phase Framework (WFPF) sets out the requirement that 'children should as far as possible be able to move freely between the indoors and outdoors' (DCELLS, 2008). Supporting guidance advocates play and 'first-hand experiences' as fundamentally important for the development of language, concentration, concepts and skills 'that will support their future learning' (DCELLS, 2008a).

Furthermore, the Northern Ireland Curricular Guidance for Pre-School Education (NIC) identifies outdoor learning as 'an integral part of the overall educational programme' and promotes a 'planned, purposeful, flexible' approach to teaching and learning where children should be given 'opportunities to explore, experiment, plan and make decisions for themselves' (CCEA,

2006). This is further supported in the Primary Curriculum, which promotes play as the main vehicle for learning in the foundation stage because children best 'develop literacy and numeracy skills in meaningful contexts' (CCEA, 2007).

Learning in the early years is about gaining the fundamental knowledge and skills that provide the basis for future learning. The outdoor environment is an ideal arena for teaching early maths, science and literacy because it offers scope to plan concrete experiences in purposeful contexts, helping children to develop a basic conceptual understanding of these subjects.

About this book

Developing Early Maths Skills Outdoors considers all aspects of mathematics including number, calculation, shape, space and measures. It is divided into the following sections:

- A sense of number and number order
- Counting
- Recognising numbers
- Recording numbers
- Comparing quantities
- Adding
- Subtracting
- Multiplying and dividing
- Problem solving
- Shape
- Pattern
- Space
- Length
- Weight
- Capacity and volume
- Time
- Money.

Each of these aspects is introduced with an explanation of why it is important, together with an overview of the fundamental concepts and skills that underpin it. This is followed up with:

- General reminders and tips about teaching early maths skills, as well as ideas for how to involve parents.

- Ideas for adult-led and adult-initiated outdoor activities that aim to develop children's early knowledge, skills and understanding in mathematics.

- Suggestions for how to enhance continuous outdoor provision so that it supports child-initiated learning that leads to a developing understanding of each particular aspect of maths.

- The main areas of learning addressed in the English, Scottish, Welsh and Northern Irish early years curriculum frameworks.*

At the end of the book there is advice on planning and organising outdoor learning with suggestions for how to make the most of different sized outside spaces. This is followed by guidance on how to collect evidence of children's learning with practical tips for observing outdoors and pointers for how to make observation less onerous. Furthermore, there is an example observation sheet together with advice on the effective use of observations to inform assessment and future planning.

Finally, there is a list of suppliers where many of the resources used for activities throughout the book can be found, as well as links to useful websites and suggestions for further reading about teaching and learning maths outdoors.

There is a large body of contemporary research highlighting the benefits of learning outdoors. Helen Bilton (2010) provides a summary:

Physical development
Research highlights links between physical exercise and cognitive development. Exercise increases the ability of blood cells to absorb oxygen and this has a positive knock-on effect for physical brain function.

Health and wellbeing
There is evidence to suggest that spending time outside in the fresh air helps to reduce illness, such as coughs and colds. Furthermore, sunlight activates vitamin D within the body, which is essential for healthy bone growth. Vitamin D can help reduce the chance of cancer and heart disease, which are also linked to sedentary lifestyles. When children are outside they are more active and get more physical exercise, which has health benefits for later life. What's more, exercise reduces stress and improves mood, which in turn boosts motivation and learning.

Learning
Studies highlight the importance of daylight and fresh air for effective learning. Many classrooms have unhealthy levels of carbon dioxide, which impacts upon children's concentration and memory. Children are more able to hear teachers and each other when they are in open spaces, making a quieter outdoor environment more conducive to learning than a noisy classroom. Furthermore, the outdoor environment is more physically challenging and this presents children with opportunities to weigh up physical risk in relation to their own capabilities. Such skills are transferable and applicable to emotional risk, giving children the courage to take on academic and philosophical challenges.

*The motor skills that children need, to be able to make marks and record numbers, are listed under 'physical development' in the EYFS, NIC and WFPF, and 'health and wellbeing' in the SCE. Therefore, additional learning outcomes from these areas of learning are indicated in brackets in the Recording numbers section of this book.

Research shows that spending time outdoors has a positive effect on children's physical development, health, well-being and general learning.

A sense of number and number order

A sense of number is important because it provides the initial foundation for constructing future mathematical understanding. Children need to understand what numbers are and be able to use them in an everyday context before they can move on in their learning. In addition, knowledge of number order and being able to recite numbers in the correct sequence helps children to count accurately. This is essential for being able to quantify and calculate later on.

A sense of number and knowledge of number order is underpinned by the following concepts:

- Knowing that numbers have meaning

- Knowing that each number has a name

- Knowing that zero is a number

- Knowing that each number follows the next in a specific sequence

- Understanding that no matter which number you start from, the order remains the same

- Knowing that numbers 13 to 19 end in 'teen'

- Knowing that multiples of 10 end in 'ty'.

Children learn about number order by reciting numbers in sequence. This usually involves singing counting rhymes and songs on a daily basis. Of course when children are outside they can sing louder and have more room to add physical actions. However, the outdoors also presents opportunities to combine physical movement with counting, which is not only fun but helps to embed knowledge of number order.

Activity 1: March to the beat

Type of activity: Adult-led, whole group.

Resources: A wide open space.

What to do: Instruct the children to find a space and march on the spot. Establish a rhythm by singing *The Grand Old Duke of York*. At the end of the song count to 10, stop and salute. Repeat a few times then encourage the children to join in a line and march around the space in single file, each time counting to 10, stopping and saluting at the end of the song.

Key vocabulary: Numbers to 10.

Extension ideas: March with a drum. Count to 20.

Use rhythm and rhyme to reinforce knowledge of number order.

Make some noise!

Activity 3: Shout it out

Type of activity: Adult-led, whole group.

Resources: A wide open space.

What to do: Ask the children to find a space and crouch down into a ball. Encourage them to count to 10 starting with a quiet voice, then gradually unfolding their bodies, and getting louder as the numbers get higher in value until they reach ten with a shout and a jump. Then get them to count back down from 10 to zero, starting with a very loud voice and gradually getting quieter as the numbers get lower in value. This time they should start standing and fold themselves down until they are in a ball again.

Key vocabulary: Numbers to 10.

Extension ideas: Start counting on and back from random numbers. Extend the counting to reach 20.

Activity 2: Number rockets

Type of activity: Adult-led, whole group.

Resources: A wide open space.

What to do: Ask the children to find a space. Explain they are going to pretend to be rockets and show them how to stand tall with their arms stretched up above them to a form a point. Tell them you are going to count down from 10 and when you reach zero they should shout 'BLAST OFF' and run into another space. Encourage the children to join in the count down. Practise a few times, then choose volunteers to come to the front and count down.

Key vocabulary: Numbers to 10.

Extension ideas: Practise starting the count down from different numbers.

HOME LINKS

Ask parents to help their children develop a sense of number and number order during everyday outdoor activities. Give examples such as pointing out how many cars there are in a busy car park, working out the number of sandwiches needed to go around everyone at a picnic and guessing how many thousands of pebbles there are on a beach.

Make the most of outdoor space.

Activity 4: Get it right

Type of activity: Adult-led, whole group.

Resources: A wide open space.

What to do: Get the children to spread out and practise doing some star jumps. Explain you would like the children to do star jumps while you count to 10 and every time they notice a mistake, they should sit on the floor. Repeat this activity several times, missing out random numbers.

Key vocabulary: Numbers to 10.

Extension ideas: Extend the counting to 20. Count backwards.

Try...

...typing question prompts, laminating them and sticking them to the inside of windows so they face out into the outside space. Practitioners can refer to these when involving children in mathematical conversations.

Activity 5: Race to finish

Type of activity: Adult-led, small groups of five.

Resources: A wide open space, rubber eggs and spoons, bucket stilts, bean bags.

What to do: Set up a variety of races that involve using different skills and will therefore result in different winners. Some examples include, running, walking, egg and spoon, walking on bucket stilts and balancing beanbags on heads. At the end of each race talk about which child came first, second, third, fourth and fifth.

Key vocabulary: Race, first, second, third, fourth and fifth.

Extension ideas: Invite more children to race and introduce sixth, seventh, eighth, ninth and tenth places.

Activity 6: All in order

Type of activity: Adult-led, groups of 10.

Resources: A large open space.

What to do: This activity may take some practice because the children have to be able to remember their number.

Begin by arranging the children in a line. Walk down the line and pat each child on the head giving them a number from one to 10. Return to the start and walk down the line again. This time tell the children to say their number when you pat them on the head. The children should count to 10. Ask them to go and find a space. Explain when you call out 'one', the child whose number is one should come to the front. When you call out 'two' the child whose number is two should come out, and so on up to 10. Call out the numbers in order and form a number line of children.

Key vocabulary: Numbers to 10.

Extension ideas: Send the children off into a space. Explain when you clap your hands you want number one to shout 'one' and start a new line. Number two should then shout 'two' and join the line, and so on until the line is formed again.

Include observations about number in everyday conversations.

Enhancing continuous provision

As well as adult-led physical games and activities that teach children about number order, practitioners should look out for opportunities to help children develop a sense of number during everyday conversations. At this stage it is not about counting accurately but making children familiar with numbers by giving them meaning and putting them into context. The outdoor environment is an ideal setting for starting such conversations. Children will generally be involved in physical activities that involve handling and moving groups and sets of objects. What's more, they are fascinated by natural objects and very much enjoy making collections of stones, seeds and sticks and using them to create patterns and constructions. All of these activities present opportunities to talk about number.

Area of provision	Enhancements that help develop a sense of number
Water	Cups and containers: Talking about how many cups it takes to fill a bucket. Aprons: Mentioning how many water aprons are left. Boats: Pointing out how many boats have sunk or tipped over and how many are still floating.
Sand	Shells and pebbles: Pointing out how many each child has in their hand. Buckets: Talking about how many buckets of sand have been used to make a castle. Children: Pointing out how many children can fit around the tray at one time.
Construction	Blocks: Pointing out how many blocks there are in a tower and asking how many bricks a child would like. Sticks: Suggesting how many sticks might be needed to make a den. Buildings: Looking at brick buildings and guessing how many thousand bricks they took to build.
Role Play	Mobile phones: Giving a child the phone number for a window cleaner. Cars/bikes: Reading out number plates, talking about how far the drive is in distance and time, pointing out how many wheels each vehicle has. Clocks: Talking about what time the cafe opens, how long it takes to get to the shops, when tea is on the table or what time the next patient is due in.
Investigation	Magnifiers: Pointing out how many magnifiers there are in relation to children. Microscope: Explaining there is only one microscope so everyone will need to take turns. Clipboards: Deciding how many clipboards will be needed for children to make notes.
Physical	Skittles: Pointing out how many skittles have been knocked over. Balls: Guessing how many balls there are in a tub. Skipping ropes: Celebrating how many skips a child achieves. Climbing frames: Pointing out how many slides or swings there are or how many children are waiting to have a turn.
Garden	Minibeasts: Pointing out how many worms or woodlice there are under a log. Puddles: Mentioning how many children have remembered their wellies. Trees: Guessing how many thousand leaves there might be on a tree.

Curriculum links

Learning about number and number order covers the following areas of learning and development:

EYFS	Recites numbers in order to 10 and back; uses some number names and number language spontaneously.
NIC	Counts forwards and backwards in ones within 5/10 from different starting points; explores ordinal number.
SCE	Explores numbers and understands they represent quantities; uses them to count, creates sequences and describes order.
WFPF	Develops an interest in numbers; uses numbers in play and daily activities; counts and orders numbers.

Counting

Counting is an essential skill that we continually use throughout each and every day, for instance when shopping, driving, cooking, eating and sharing things out. Being able to count accurately is the precursor to quantifying and calculating.

Counting involves the following skills and concepts:

- Being able to recite number names in order

- Using one-to-one correspondence (counting one object at a time and linking each object to a number)

- Remembering which object you started counting from

- Counting in a logical sequence so as not to count an object twice

- Knowing that the number said on the last object is the total amount in the group

- Understanding that anything can be counted including claps, jumps and sounds

- Understanding that zero represents a set of nothing.

Children learn to count through practice, as well as by singing counting rhymes and sharing picture books. Of course such opportunities can be presented outside by placing counting books in a tent or on a comfortable rug and initiating the singing of number rhymes while working in the garden.

However, the outdoor environment also offers plenty of unique opportunities to plan meaningful activities that give children a reason to count.

Activity 1: Sand creatures

Type of activity: Adult-initated, during independent play.

Resources: Plastic bugs, frogs and scorpions, bucket, three containers, sieves, spades.

What to do: Bury a selection of plastic bugs, frogs and scorpions in the sand pit or tray. Challenge the children to dig up as many creatures as they can and provide a bucket for them to put the creatures in. Ask the children to count out how many creatures they have found in total. Then give them three containers and ask them to sort the creatures and count how many there are of each.

Key vocabulary: Find, count, sort, numbers to 20, how many?

Extension ideas: Add more creatures.

Make counting meaningful and fun.

Activity 2: Mud pies

Type of activity: Adult-initiated, during independent play.

Resources: Pots, pans, wooden spoons, cups, jugs, measuring spoons, ladles, laminated recipe cards.

What to do: Set up a cooking area for children to make mud pies. Make and laminate some pictorial recipe cards that encourage children to count out quantities of ingredients. Put a picture of each ingredient, for example, soil, sand, water, grass, acorns and leaves. Then next to the ingredient put the corresponding measure using pictures of cups, spoons, jugs or ladles. This will encourage the children to count the measuring utensils on the cards and then count out the actual measures while making their mud pies.

Key vocabulary: Numbers to 10, measure, count, ingredients, enough, more, less, how many?

Extension ideas: Provide clipboards, paper and pencils for the children to make up their own recipes. Provide templates featuring pictures of key ingredients and leave space for the children to draw how many cups or spoons of each they have used.

Activity 3: How many steps?

Type of activity: Adult-led, small groups of up to five children.

Resources: Large tarmacked area, playground chalk, clipboard, paper, pen.

What to do: Use playground chalk to draw out a large-scale plan of a treasure island on the floor. Draw a pirate ship at the edge of the island to mark the starting point. Then draw landmarks on the island including a palm tree, large skull-shaped rock, beach hut and lake. Put a big X somewhere. Work with one group of children first. Explain you would like them to work out how many steps it takes to reach the X. Invite one child to walk from the ship to the first landmark, the palm tree for instance, counting his steps as he goes. Write the first instruction down, take 10 steps to palm tree point. Ask the next child to walk from the palm tree to the rock, again counting his steps. Write down the next instruction, take 8 steps to skull rock. Continue until you have a full set of instructions. Bring another group to the 'island' and ask individuals to follow the instructions and count their steps from one landmark to the next until they locate the treasure.

Key vocabulary: Steps, count, numbers to 10, how many?

Extension ideas: Allow the children to play on the 'island' and challenge them to plan out different routes to the treasure.

HOME LINKS

Ask parents to help their children develop counting skills by singing number rhymes during car journeys, reading counting books when out on a picnic and counting everyday objects when at the beach, park or supermarket. Suggest they collect objects such as pebbles, shells, pinecones and conkers for their children to sort and count when playing outside.

Make-believe maths.

Activity 5: Daisy chains

Type of activity: Adult-led, small groups.

Resources: Grassy area where daisies grow, timer.

What to do: Challenge the children to make the longest daisy chains they can in a set amount of time. Many will need help joining the daisies together. Dandelions are sometimes easier for small hands. When the time is up bring the children together to count how many daisies they have in their chains. Talk about who has more/less daisies.

Key vocabulary: Join, count, numbers to 10, how many?

Extension ideas: Count the petals on some daisies to find out if they all have the same or different amounts. Look around for different flowers and count how many petals they have.

Find inspiration in nature to count.

Activity 4: Alien invasion

Type of activity: Adult-initiated, during independent play.

Resources: Cardboard box, craft materials, scissors, glue, sellotape, green water soluble paint, 20 toy aliens.

What to do: Use a cardboard box and craft materials to make an alien space craft. Cut out a door and open it slightly. Wedge the craft into a tree or somewhere high up so the children cannot touch it. Cut out a selection of different shaped footprints from thick card. Dip these into green paint and put some footprints leading in various directions from the area just below the craft. Then hide toy aliens all over the outdoor area. When the children discover the crash site ask them what they think has happened. Can they guess how many aliens might have run away? Encourage the children to search the area, find and count the aliens.

Key vocabulary: Count, numbers to 20, how many?

Extension ideas: Set up a role-play alien shelter. Ask the children to count out how many beds, blankets, cups and plates they need to provide for the aliens.

Don't forget to think about...

...the fact that we can count anything. This includes claps, jumps, drum beats and sounds, as well as tangible objects.

Activity 6: Back of the net

Type of activity: Adult-led, small groups.

Resources: A large space, football goal (otherwise use two chairs as markers), 10 footballs, large tub.

What to do: Set up a football goal and place a large tub containing 10 footballs a reasonable distance away. Invite one child at a time to have a go at kicking all 10 footballs into the goal. Then approach the goal and count how many balls went in and how many missed.

Key vocabulary: Aim, kick, goal, miss, numbers to 10, count, how many?

Extension ideas: Increase the number of balls. Also, it is likely that if a child only scores five they will know how many balls there are on sight. Therefore, if there are only a few balls in the goal ask more able children if they can tell you how many balls went in without counting.

Enhancing continuous provision

There are many resources that can be provided to encourage children to practise counting skills during their play. Below are suggestions for loose items that children can collect, sort, arrange and count. There are also ideas for resources that will help and encourage them to do so.

Join the children as they play, model counting and ask 'how many?' questions. Make question cards that can be laminated and displayed in the different areas of provision that practitioners can refer to as prompts. Again there are ideas in the table below for different types of questions that will encourage children to count.

Area of provision	Enhancements that encourage children to practise counting
Water	Provide cups, jugs, ladles, fish, boats, sea monsters, mermaids, glass pebbles, rubber ducks, nets, corks, plastic bottle tops. Question ideas: How many pebbles can you fish out with your net? Can you make seven splashes in the water?
Sand	Provide coins, pebbles, shells, buckets, scoops, bugs and creatures, buttons, dinosaur bones, fossils, gems, jewels, cotton reels. Question ideas: How many scoops of sand do you need to fill the bucket? How many coins have you found?
Construction	Provide bricks, blocks, boxes, small tyres, rocks, wheelbarrows, trolleys, large trucks. Question ideas: Can you count how many bricks there are in the tower? How many wheels does this truck have?
Role Play	Camping: Provide crockery, cutlery, pegs, sleeping bags, torches, tinned foods. Market stall: Provide coins, food items, paper bags, bucket scales, scoops. Garage: Provide buckets, sponges, money, cars, trikes. Question ideas: How many tins of food have you got in your bag? Can you give me four scoops of beans please? How many cars are in the garage today?
Investigation	Provide sorting tubs, jars, containers, bags. Display laminated question cards featuring 'how many?' questions, for example, How many dinosaur bones can you find buried in the soil? How many cars can you see driving past? or How many brown/red/yellow leaves can you find?
Physical	Provide balls, cones, quoits, hula hoops, beanbags, large bricks and blocks, stepping stones, skipping ropes. Provide percussion instruments for a marching band, including drums, tambourines, pots, pans and wooden spoons.
Garden	Provide seeds, bulbs, seed trays, flower pots, labels, pinecones, feathers, leaves, acorns, conkers, chestnuts, sycamore seeds, stones, flowers, sticks. Question ideas: How many pinecones have you collected? How many bulbs have you planted? How many labels do you need?

Curriculum links

Learning to count accurately covers the following areas of learning and development:

EYFS	Knows that numbers identify how many objects are in a set; realises not only objects, but anything can be counted; counts objects to 10 and beyond by saying one number name for each item.
NIC	Counts a variety of objects; understands one-to-one correspondence and appreciates that the size of a set is given by the last number in the count; develops an understanding of the conservation of number; states without counting quantities within 5; extends when appropriate counting in ones beyond 10.
SCE	Develops a sense of size and amount by exploring, observing and using; explores numbers and understands they represent quantities; uses them to count.
WFPF	Uses numbers in play and daily activities; counts and appreciates the conservation of number.

Recognising numbers

Numbers are everywhere and used to represent meaning in a wide range of everyday contexts including dates, times, addresses, phone numbers, television channels, recipes, prices and distances.

Being able to recognise numbers is an absolutely essential skill for being able to function within society at the most basic level. It is also important for progression in mathematical thinking, making it possible to label quantities and read and record calculations.

Recognising numbers involves understanding the following concepts:

- Knowing that numbers are represented by numerals

- Knowing that zero is a number

- Understanding that numbers can have one, two, three or more digits

- Recognising that numerals 1, 7, 4 and 9 look different when presented in various fonts and handwriting.

Children learn to recognise numbers through regular and frequent exposure to them. Most early years settings will have an indoor maths area that is decorated with number charts and posters and filled with maths resources for the children to play and experiment with. However, it is just as important to create a number rich outdoor environment and plan activities that involve children reading and playing with numbers. Active outdoor games that involve number recognition make this so much more fun.

Activity 1: Natural number line

Type of activity: Adult-initiated, during independent play.

Resources: 11 large containers, marker pen or number cards and sellotape.

What to do: Stick or draw numbers zero to 10 onto a set of large containers. Invite some children to arrange the containers in numerical order to create a number line. Challenge the children to go scavenging and fill the containers with the correct number of natural items.

Key vocabulary: Numbers to 10, count, too many, not enough, more, less, how many?

Extension ideas: Every now and then mix up the order of the containers and mix up the contents. Ask volunteers to come and sort out the mess.

Find fun ways to play with numbers.

HOME LINKS

Ask parents to help their children recognise numbers by pointing out numerals in the local environment, for example, on road signs, doors, vehicle number plates, bus tickets and price tags. Suggest they provide a toy or old mobile phone for their children to use during role-play outside.

Activity 3: Number hop

Type of activity: Adult-led, whole group.

Resources: Large cards showing numbers zero to 10.

What to do: Take the children to a large space and ask them to spread out. Explain you are going to hold up a number card and shout an action. The children must then do the action the number of times it says on the card. For example, hold up number five and shout hop. The children must then hop five times. Repeat holding up different number cards and shouting instructions such as stamp, star-jump, clap and wave. Explain they should stand still if you hold up number zero. Help the children by doing the actions with them whilst counting out loud.

Key vocabulary: Numbers 10, count, which number? how many times?

Extension ideas: Bring children out to the front to choose the cards and hold them up. Ask these children to shout out an instruction linked to the number they have picked. For example, 'wave three times'.

Activity 2: Roll and run

Type of activity: Adult-led, small groups.

Resources: Playground chalk, large spotted dice.

What to do: Draw six large circles on the floor of a big open space, ensuring they are spread well apart. Label the circles one to six. Invite a small group of children to come and play. Explain the children must roll the dice and run to the correct numbered circle. Give one child a large dice and ask them to roll it and count the spots. Once the child says the total number, the children must wait for you to shout, 'Ready, steady, go!' before running to the correct circle.

Key vocabulary: Numbers to 6, count, run, which number? how many?

Extension ideas: Draw more circles featuring numbers seven to 12 and introduce a second dice with sides showing seven to 12 spots. Introduce a circle labeled zero and adapt one of the dice so that it has a blank side.

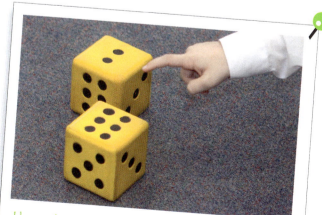
Use a dice to enhance outdoor number play.

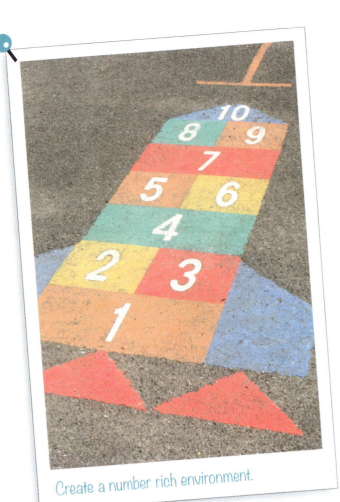

Create a number rich environment.

Activity 4: Cork it

Type of activity: Adult-initiated, during independent play.

Resources: 11 plastic sand-filled bottles, 11 corks, permanent marker, fishing nets, water tray.

What to do: Write numbers zero to 10 on a set of corks in permanent marker, then do the same on the bottles. Stand the bottles next to the water tray and throw the corks in the water. Challenge the children to fish the corks out, stick them in the corresponding bottles and arrange the bottles in numerical order.

Key vocabulary: Numbers to 10, which number? match, order, count.

Extension ideas: Increase the number of bottles and corks to 20. Leave some corks out and ask the children to work out which are missing. Use empty bottles and challenge the children to put the correct number of stones in each.

Don't forget to think about...

...presenting numbers in different styles to help children recognise numerals in a range of fonts and handwriting.

Activity 5: Sycamore wheel

Type of activity: Adult-led, small groups.

Resources: Playground chalk, sycamore seeds.

What to do: Collect a good amount of large sycamore seeds. If possible, take the children out to collect some themselves. Leave the seeds somewhere to dry out. Use playground chalk to draw a large circle on a tarmacked floor and divide the circle up into eight or 10 sections (like pizza slices). Write a number in each section; this can be numbers one to eight/10, zero to seven/nine or just random numbers that you know the children are unsure of.

Take the sycamore seeds outside with a small group of children. Invite one child at a time to stand in the centre of the circle and throw their seed in the air. Watch it twirl to the floor and ask the children to identify which number it has landed on.

Key vocabulary: Numbers to 10, which number?

Extension ideas: Give each child a handful of seeds to throw all at once. Watch where the seeds land and ask the children to tell you how many seeds landed on each number, which number the most/least seeds landed on, which numbers the seeds did not land on at all, and so on.

Activity 6: Number hunt

Type of activity: Adult-led, small groups.

Resources: Plastic or wooden numbers zero to 10.

What to do: Hide a set of numbers all around the outdoor area. Send a small group of children off to find them, bring them back and arrange them to form a number line. When the line is complete ask the children to take the numbers and hide them ready for the next group.

Key vocabulary: Numbers to 10, arrange, order.

Extension ideas: Go out for a walk and look for numbers in the local environment, for example, door numbers, road signs, town hall clocks, bus/train timetables and price lists. Talk about how big or small the numbers are. Point out how many digits each number has. Explain that two-digit numbers should be read as 'twelve' or 'nineteen', not 'one-two' or 'one-nine'. Point out the difference between some handwritten numerals on shop signs and printed numerals on doors or car number plates, for example.

Enhancing continuous provision

To help children recognise numbers it is important to create a number rich environment. The outdoors is ideal for physical number play. Paint number tracks on the floor and targets on the walls and provide giant dice for children to make up their own games. Print and laminate large number cards and provide playground chalks for children to have a go at writing

numerals themselves. There is a wide selection of numbered resources on the market, ranging from squidgy gel filled numbers to natural wooden discs with numbers carved in. Place these around the outdoor area for children to play with. Otherwise create some resources by yourself using a marker pen to write numbers on balls, beanbags and bricks.

Area of provision	Enhancements that help children to recognise numbers
Water	Provide inflatable numbers, squidgy sparkle numbers and rubber numbers. Paint numbers on fish, boats, rubber ducks, nets, bottles, cups and jugs. Drop small objects into the water and provide numbered sorting tubs. Use number ice moulds and food colouring to make frozen numbers.
Sand	Provide number shaped sand moulds and numbered sandcastle flags. Paint numbers on shells, pebbles and buckets. Bury small objects and provide numbered sorting tubs.
Construction	Write numbers on bricks, hard hats, buckets, tabards and wheelbarrows. Provide large rubber number tiles to use as flooring.
Role Play	Stick number plates on cars and trikes, draw out numbered parking bays and make road signs featuring speed limits and directions to local roads (the A6 for example). Put door numbers on playhouses and provide mobile phones. Provide tills, receipts and numbered coins for use on a market stall. Use banana boxes to make a train; number the carriages and station platforms, and write phone numbers on luggage tags.
Investigation	Provide numbered sorting tubs and containers. Provide clipboards, pencils and numbered charts for children to fill in. Make laminated number cards that children can use as labels.
Physical	Paint or draw number snakes, number squares and hopscotch games on the floor. Paint or draw targets on the wall with a numbered scoring system. Provide numbered balls, beanbags, hoops, bats, quoits and large dice.
Garden	Paint number lines from 0 to 20 on fencing and walls. Paint numbers on stepping stones and stairways. Put door numbers on sheds and gates. Provide numbered baskets for collecting natural items. Hang numbered bunting, put numbered flags and windmills around and about.

Curriculum links

Learning to recognise numbers covers the following areas of learning and development:

EYFS	Shows an interest in numerals in the environment; selects the correct numeral to represent 1 to 5, then 1 to 10 objects.
NIC	Recognises numerals up to 5/10; matches numerals to sets; extends when appropriate recognition of numbers beyond 10.
SCE	Explores numbers and understands they represent quantities; uses numbers to count, creates sequences and describes order; understands the importance of zero.
WFPF	Uses number names accurately, matching the symbol to the sound; reads numbers; uses numbers naturally in play; observes numbers in the environment and everyday life.

Recording numbers

Being able to record numbers is important because it enables children to organise their mathematical thinking. Recording numbers is not just about the formation of numerals. Children engage in mathematical mark-making to help them make sense of number, for example by including numbers that are familiar to them in their drawings. They also keep note of quantities, using tally marks for instance, which is the beginning of more complex thinking that leads to calculating and solving problems.

Recording numbers involves the following skills and concepts:

● Being able to recognise numerals and numbers

● Being able to hold and use a mark-making tool

● Knowing that marks carry meaning and can sometimes represent numbers

● Knowing that numbers are represented by numerals

● Understanding that numbers can be represented by sets of objects.

Children learn about the purpose of recording numbers by watching others engage in mathematical mark-making.

Writing and recording is not just an indoor exercise. The outdoors provides the space for children to practise the correct formation of numerals before they have the fine motor control to record on paper. What's more, there are many outdoor activities that present purposeful opportunities for recording numbers. The following activities involve adults demonstrating the purpose of mathematical record keeping then providing the tools for children to do their own.

Activity 1: Muddy marks

Type of activity: Adult-led, small groups.

Resources: Large patch of mud, large number cards zero to nine, large sheets of paper, bowl of warm soapy water, towel.

What to do: Get the children to take their shoes and socks off and create foot print numerals.

Ask each child to choose a number card, dip their feet in the mud and form muddy numeral shapes by walking on large sheets of paper.

Key vocabulary: Numbers zero to nine, numeral, number, write, form.

Extension ideas: Provide number moulds to make mud numbers. Press stones or pebbles into the mud to create numerals. Use sticks to write numerals in the mud.

Record numbers for a purpose.

Activity 3: Nature pictogram

Type of activity: Adult-initiated, small groups.

Resources: Playground chalks, timer.

What to do: Use playground chalks to mark out a large chart on the floor. Draw pictures of natural objects in the first column, for example conkers, leaves, twigs, daisies and stones. Send the children off to collect as many of these items as they can in the space of five or 10 minutes. When they return ask them to lay their objects next to the corresponding picture on the chart to create a pictogram. Count the objects and write the totals at the end of each row.

Key vocabulary: Collect, count, how many? total, chart, pictogram.

Extension ideas: Give the children some chalks to use and encourage them to create their own pictograms out of other natural objects and toys.

Activity 2: Post it

Type of activity: Adult-initiated, during independent play.

Resources: Very large cardboard boxes, large decorators' paint brushes, coloured poster paint, permanent marker, watered down PVA glue, gaffer tape, sharp knife, envelopes, postcards, pens, fake postage stamps, postal worker uniforms, post bags.

What to do: Make a street of cardboard box houses. Use a sharp knife to cut out front doors and windows. Lift the flaps on the top of the boxes and gaffer tape them into a roof shape. Provide large paint brushes and invite the children to help paint the walls brown, roofs grey and doors nice bright colours. When dry, use a marker pen to draw on bricks and roof tiles. Write a number on each door and cut out letterboxes. Coat the houses in watered down PVA glue to make them more durable and damp proof. Provide role-play postal uniforms and bags, as well as envelopes and postcards that are already addressed and a good supply of blank ones for the children to address themselves.

Key vocabulary: Numbers to 10, house number, postal area, postcode.

Extension ideas: Talk about postal areas and why postcodes are used. Look at the postcode of the setting. Identify the numbers and letters. Help the children create a postcode for their role-play street and encourage them to add postcodes to their letters. Send some real letters.

Use the open space to practise numeral formation.

Activity 5: Ribbon writing

Type of activity: Adult-initiated, during independent play.

Resources: Open space, playground chalks, ribbon wands.

What to do: In very large writing write numerals zero to nine on the floor outside. Use a different colour to add some small guiding arrows to indicate correct formation. Invite children to come and write the numbers in the air using ribbon wands. Join in and demonstrate the correct formation.

Key vocabulary: Numbers to nine, numeral, number, write, form.

Extension ideas: Give the children the chalks to practise writing the numerals on the floor.

Strengthen arms and hands to improve fine motor control.

Activity 4: Keeping track

Type of activity: Adult-initiated, during independent play.

Resources: Crate or large blocks, plank of wood or piece of guttering, playground chalk, easel, paper, pens.

What to do: Set up a ramp. At the base use playground chalk to draw five evenly spaced horizontal lines and label them one to five. Then set up an easel displaying a chart with numbers one to five in the first column.

Provide a tub of small vehicles and choose a child to set a vehicle off at the top of the ramp and see how far it travels. Show the child how to put a mark on the chart next to the line that the vehicle reaches. Allow the children to take it in turns to set different vehicles off down the slope and record which line they reached. Look at the chart with the children. Count how many times the vehicles reached line number two. Ask the children how many times the vehicles reached line number three. Can they tell you which line the most vehicles have reached? Have any vehicles been able to reach line number five?

Key vocabulary: How far? distance, line number, mark, record.

Extension ideas: Provide clipboards and pens with blank charts for the children to use when making up their own games.

Activity 6: Keeping score

Type of activity: Adult-led, small groups.

Resources: Large piece of card, marker pen, photos of children, football goal, footballs.

What to do: Prepare a score board for each set of children using named photos. Set up a football goal and invite each child to kick three balls into the goal. After each child has had their turn record their score next to their picture on the score board using tally marks. Allow each child to have three turns before tallying up the final scores and writing these in numerals on the board.

Key vocabulary: Score, tally, mark, how many? how many altogether? most, winner.

Extension ideas: Make a set of blank scoring cards for the children to write their own names on and record their scores while playing independently.

Enhancing continuous provision

When outside children have the chance to practise large and small movements, helping them to develop both gross motor skills and fine motor control. This is vital preparation for being able to use writing implements later on. Therefore, it is important to set up an outdoor learning environment that encourages children to make controlled movements that help improve coordination.

In addition, children will have ready access to pens, pencils and paper when inside. However, it is just as possible to encourage them to write and draw outdoors if presented with the appropriate resources. The ideas in the table below demonstrate how this can be further extended to encourage mathematical mark-making by placing writing equipment in particular areas and near certain activities.

Area of provision	Enhancements that encourage mark-making and recording numbers
Water	Provide buckets and large paint brushes for 'painting' on walls. Put a cornflour and water mix in the tray for children to make disappearing marks using their fingers, sticks or laces, for example.
Sand	Add a little water to make the sand damp and provide objects that the children can draw with, including sticks, rakes and clay sculpting tools. Provide number stamps for making prints in the sand.
Construction	Provide clipboards with ready made charts featuring pictures of objects that can be counted, including bricks, hard hats and tools. Provide tape measures, notepads and pens for recording measurements. Provide paper, pencils and rulers for children to draw plans.
Role Play	Provide address books, telephone books, train/bus timetables, cookery books, calendars, notebooks, notepads, post-it notes, pens and pencils for children to record house numbers, phone numbers, train times and recipe ingredients, for example, during their play.
Investigation	Set up investigations that encourage children to test and record. For example, Find out how many balls bounce or Find out how many metal objects are magnetic. Set up an easel or provide clipboards for them to record their results.
Physical	Set up an easel with score board next to games equipment. Provide clipboards, paper and pens for recording scores. Provide playground chalks for the children to draw out number wheels, race tracks, number squares and hopscotches.
Garden	Provide clipboards, paper and pens, lolly sticks, seed packets with expiry dates, numbered seed trays and plant pots. Provide compost, number shaped cookie cutters and cress seeds to grow cress numbers. Set up a large tally chart featuring minibeasts for children to record tally marks whenever they spot something.

Curriculum links

Learning to record numbers covers the following areas of learning and development:

EYFS	Begins to represent numbers using fingers, marks on paper or pictures; records, making marks that they can interpret and explain. Shows control in holding and using mark-making tools (PD); draws lines and circles using gross motor movements (PD); begins to use anticlockwise movements and retraces vertical lines (PD).
NIC	Uses appropriate mathematical language and symbols; records outcomes in a variety of ways; talks about data represented in simple tables and diagrams. Handles small tools with increasing control (PD).
SCE	Explores interesting materials for writing and different ways of recording ideas and information; creates a range of visual information through observing and recording from experiences across the curriculum. Is learning to move body well, exploring how to manage and control it (HW); is developing movement skills through practice and energetic play (HW).
WFPF	Presents work pictorially and in written form, moving on to using more formal methods of recording when developmentally ready; reads and writes numbers. Develops coordination, gross motor skills and fine manipulative skills (PD).

Comparing quantities

Being able to compare quantities by looking at sets of objects and deciding which is larger or smaller, is the precursor to calculating. When children add more items to increase a quantity they are adding. When they look at the difference between sets of objects they are learning about subtraction. When they share objects out and look at who has got more or less they are playing with division. What's more, when they double the number of skittles in a game they are using multiplication.

Comparing quantities involves the following skills and concepts:

- Understanding and being able to use language such as 'same', 'more' and 'less' to describe and compare quantities

- Understanding that adding more and multiplying increases a quantity

- Understanding that taking away and dividing decreases a quantity

- Being able to recognise larger/smaller amounts

- Being able to count accurately.

Children learn to compare quantities through play and practical activities that involve sorting, comparing and counting. Practitioners help by engaging children in conversation and introducing mathematical vocabulary that will help them to verbalise their own thinking.

As well as making use of the plentiful natural resources that can be found all around us outside, the following activities also take advantage of the outdoor space where children can play messy games and compare quantities on a larger scale.

Activity 1: Dump it

Type of activity: Adult-initiated, during independent play.

Resources: Toy dumper trucks, pebbles, large stones.

What to do: Set up a small world building site with a range of toy dumper trucks, stones and pebbles. Join in the children's play. Load up a dumper truck with pebbles and talk about how many you can fit in the back. Fill a different sized truck. Compare the two, talking about which truck can carry the most/least pebbles. Ask the children if they think their trucks could carry more or less than yours.

Key vocabulary: More, less, most, least.

Extension ideas: Extend the conversation. Ask the children if they can fit even more pebbles in their trucks. Ask them to dump some pebbles so that they have less. Count out the pebbles to check which truck holds the most/least.

Who can collect the most natural objects?

HOME LINKS

Ask parents to help their children compare quantities by involving them in outdoor activities. Give examples such as counting out how many snails there are munching the beans compared to the lettuce, how many tomatoes there are on one plant compared to another and how many windows there are on the back of the house compared to the front.

Activity 3: Blowing bubbles

Type of activity: Adult-led, small groups.

Resources: Wide open space, pots of bubble mix.

What to do: Take the children to a wide open space and get them to take turns blowing bubbles. Each time a child has a turn, encourage everyone to talk about how many bubbles they have blown. Did this child blow more or less bubbles than the last? Who managed to blow the most bubbles in one go? Who blew the least?

Key vocabulary: How many? more, less, most, least.

Extension ideas: Allow the children to have another go. Take the first turn, then challenge a child to blow more bubbles than you. Continue, challenging each child to blow more bubbles than the child before them. Each time discuss whether each child managed to blow more bubbles or if they blew less.

Activity 2: Who can find the most...?

Type of activity: Adult-led, small groups.

Resources: Small hand-held baskets, timer.

What to do: This activity is best done in a park or woodland area where there is scope to find plenty of items. Challenge the children to go and find a particular natural object in a set amount of time. When the time is up bring the children together to compare how many they have found. Look at the quantities and encourage the children to make a judgement about who has found the most/least. Count out the objects to check. Repeat the activity but this time send them in search of something different.

Key vocabulary: How many? most, least, more, less, same.

Extension ideas: Set up a score chart to record who brings back the most each time. Then at the end look at who scored the most/least points. Ask the children to share out their items so that everyone has the same.

Try...

...playing sorting games with the children. Sort them by gender, hair colour or clothing, for example, and compare the numbers in each group.

Count and compare vegetable crops.

Activity 5: Coin drop

Type of activity: Adult-led, small groups.

Resources: Plastic coins that will float, real coins, bucket

What to do: Bring the children to the water tray and show them a bucket filled with a mix of plastic and real coins. Invite a child to grab a handful of coins and drop them in the water. Wait for the coins to settle then ask the children whether more coins sank to the bottom or remained floating on the surface. Count the coins to check and reinforce by modeling the correct mathematical language, for example, 'more coins sank to the bottom than floated on the top' or 'there are fewer coins floating on top of the water than there are sitting on the bottom'. Fish all the coins out and invite another child to have a go.

Key vocabulary: More, less, same, fewer.

Extension ideas: Make it trickier by increasing the number of coins that are dropped in at any one time.

Make ice-creams and compare toppings.

Activity 4: A good crop

Type of activity: Adult-led, small groups.

Resources: Two dustbins or planting area, compost, seed potatoes, watering cans, sheltered sunny spot.

What to do: Help the children to plant and grow two crops of potatoes in two separate dustbins. When the plants are fully grown tip the bins up and have a look to see how many potatoes the plants have produced. Ask the children to look at the two crops and guess which is the biggest. Then ask them to sift out the potatoes and count them to check which crop has the most/least.

Key vocabulary: How many? most, least, more, less, count, check.

Extension ideas: Look at other plants you have grown with the children. For example, compare the crops on tomato plants or count and compare the number of petals on sunflowers.

Activity 6: Ice cream shack

Type of activity: Adult-led, small groups.

Resources: Ice cream, scoops, cones, sweet sauces, sprinkles, small sweets, table, aprons, sunbrella.

What to do: Set up an ice cream shack outside on a hot sunny day. Arrange some ice cream cones and toppers on a table under the shade of a sunbrella.

Invite a group of children to the table and bring out a tub of ice cream. Help each of them to put one scoop of ice cream into a cone, then allow them to add their own toppings. Before the children eat their ice creams, pause to have a look and compare each of the toppings. Talk about who has more/less sauce, who has the most sweets on the top and who has the least sprinkles. Point out that everyone has the same amount of ice cream.

Key vocabulary: More, less, fewer, most, least, same.

Extension ideas: Set up a role-play ice cream shack with card cones, cotton wool ice-cream and sticky gems or beads for topping sweets. Join in the play and model ordering a cone and using mathematical language to describe what you get. For example, if your cone contains just a little ice cream but lots of toppings, ask for more ice cream or explain that you would like less toppings. Compare your ice cream to the other children's.

Enhancing continuous provision

Children enjoy collecting and sorting. Therefore, it is a good idea to enhance outdoor activities with collections of small objects that they can count out and divide into sets. This will naturally lead on to comparing and quantifying. Think about providing objects that can be sorted by size, shape, colour and category. The table below contains suggestions for objects and resources that will encourage children to play in this way along with suggested questions that practitioners can use to prompt mathematical thinking.

Area of provision	Enhancements that encourage children to compare quantities
Water	Provide jugs and buckets for children to find out which buckets hold the most/least jugs of water. Make ice cubes for children to load into containers. Add different coloured water beads to the water tray for children to fish out, count and compare quantities.
Sand	Provide spades and buckets for children to find out which buckets hold the most/least spades of sand. Provide pebbles, shells, stones, dinosaur bones, gems and gold coins to dig up, count and compare quantities of each. Empty the sand tray and fill it with different coloured pasta shapes for the children to sort, count and compare quantities of each.
Construction	Provide construction sets featuring different sized and coloured pieces, Stickle Bricks or Jumbomagnetics, for example, will encourage children to compare how many of each size or colour they need. Set up an easel displaying laminated question cards, for example, Whose tower has the least/most bricks? or What might happen if you use less sticks?
Role Play	Market stall: Provide plenty of fruits and vegetables to weigh, count and compare. Garage: Provide a variety of vehicles for children to count and compare the number of wheels, doors, seats etc. Laundrette: Set up a washing line and various types of clothing for children to count and compare the number of T-shirts, skirts, trousers, socks and coloured pegs.
Investigation	Provide different sized containers and tubs for filling, counting and comparing numbers of natural objects.
Physical	Display laminated challenge cards that encourage children to count and make comparisons. For example, provide a sand timer and ask: How many times can you hop, skip and jump in one minute? or line up some plastic bottles, provide three beanbags and ask Who can knock the most bottles down in one turn?
Garden	Set up a bird hide and provide identification charts and record sheets for children to spot birds, record and compare how many they see of each. Provide bug collectors, jars and magnifiers for children to collect minibeasts, observe, count and compare aspects of their features, for example, the number of legs on a woodlouse compared to a beetle, or the numbers of spots on different ladybirds.

Curriculum links

Learning to compare quantities covers the following areas of learning and development:

EYFS	Makes comparisons between quantities; knows that a group of things changes in quantity when something is added or taken away; compares two groups of objects, saying when they have the same number; uses the language of 'more' and 'fewer' to compare two sets of objects.
NIC	Compares sets by matching objects/counting objects to understand the terms 'more than', 'less than', 'the same'.
SCE	Develops a sense of amount by observing, exploring, using and communicating with others about things in the world around them; explores numbers, understanding that they represent quantities.
WFPF	Counts and compares numbers; experiments with and observes numbers in the environment and everyday life.

Adding

Children need to have a firm grasp of number before they can understand and use calculation strategies. Being able to add, subtract, multiply and divide is important for many functional reasons and we use these calculation methods throughout our everyday lives, including when we are shopping, cooking, setting the table and organising time. Perhaps the easiest concept for young children to understand is addition.

Addition involves the following skills and concepts:

- Being able to count accurately

- Understanding that addition involves combining sets of objects together

- Understanding and being able to use language such as 'add', 'altogether', 'count on' and 'total'

- Having a secure understanding of number order

- Being able to say the number that is one more than a given number

- Knowing without counting how many there are in sets of up to five objects

- Being able to count on from a given number.

Children need to have a secure understanding of what addition means before they can move on to more formal practices. Therefore practitioners should plan opportunities for children to practise physically separating and combining sets of objects and finding out how many there are altogether before moving on to tasks that involve counting on. The following outdoor activities make this introduction to addition both fun and meaningful.

Activity 1: Dipping dinosaurs

Type of activity: Adult-led, small groups.

Resources: Grassy area, mud, six toy dinosaurs.

What to do: Stand a set of six toy dinosaurs on a grassy patch near a muddy patch. Count the dinosaurs together and say, 'There are six dinosaurs on the grass'. Invite a child to place some dinosaurs in the mud. Together count how many dinosaurs are in the mud then say, 'There are two dinosaurs in the mud'. Count how many are on the grass and say, 'There are four dinosaurs on the grass'. Then count all of the dinosaurs and say, 'There are six dinosaurs altogether'. Repeat the activity, giving each child a turn to move the dinosaurs. Explain that no matter how many dinosaurs are on the grass or in the mud each time, the total is always six.

Key vocabulary: Numbers to six, count, how many? altogether, total.

Extension ideas: Say the number sentence, 'four and two makes six altogether'.

Practise separating and combining sets of objects.

HOME LINKS

Ask parents to help their children develop an understanding of addition by involving them in mathematical conversation when doing outdoor activities. Give examples such as asking them to work out how many more plant pots they need when planting seeds or how many swings there are altogether at the local playground.

Activity 3: Conker dominoes

Type of activity: Adult-led, small groups.

Resources: Playground chalks, plentiful supply of conkers.

What to do: Draw a large blank domino on the floor. Place three conkers on one side of the domino. Choose a child and challenge her to add some conkers to the other side so the domino has a total of five spots on it. Say the number sentence, 'Three and two makes five altogether'.

Key vocabulary: Domino, add, total, altogether, how many? check, count, not enough, how many more?

Extension ideas: Place number and symbol cards under the domino to show the visual number sentence, 3 + 2 = 5.

Activity 2: Easter egg hunt

Type of activity: Adult-led, two children at a time.

Resources: 20 colourful and unbreakable eggs, timer.

What to do: Hide the eggs all over the outdoor area. Choose two children and explain they have one minute to find as many eggs as they can. When the time is up ask the children to bring their eggs over and place them in two sets on the floor. Count how many eggs one child has found and say, 'Hannah has found three eggs'. Then count how many eggs the other child has found and say, 'Adam has found two eggs'. Ask the children to push their eggs together, then count how many there and say, 'There are five eggs altogether'. Send the children to hide the eggs and choose two more children to have a go.

Key vocabulary: Count, how many? altogether.

Extension ideas: Say the number sentence, 'three and two makes five altogether'.

Use themes to inspire topical addition activities.

Use a number track to introduce the concept of counting on.

Activity 5: Marble run

Type of activity: Adult-initiated, during independent play.

Resources: Two equal lengths of pipe, 10 marbles or small balls, three tubs.

What to do: Set up the lengths of pipe so that they are on a slope running parallel to each other. Place the bottom end of each pipe into a tub to catch the marbles. Invite two children to pick up a random handful of marbles each. Ask them to stand one at the top end of each pipe and drop their marbles down. Go to the tubs at the bottom of the pipes and count how many marbles there are in each tub. Then tip both sets of marbles into another tub and count how many there are altogether.

Key vocabulary: Count, how many? altogether.

Extension ideas: Use a handheld whiteboard to write a number sentence each time, for example, '4 + 6 = 10'. Show and read it to the children.

A fun way of finding 'one more'.

Activity 4: Move along

Type of activity: Adult-led, small groups.

Resources: Playground chalk or large interconnecting number tiles zero to 10, large number cards from zero to seven, large dice with sides showing one, two and three spots.

What to do: Draw out a number track or make a number track with interconnecting number tiles. Ensure the track starts with number zero. Choose one child to pick a number card and go and stand on the corresponding number on the track. Invite another child to roll the dice. The child on the track must then jump forward the correct number of spaces. So for example, if the child picked card number five, they must start on number five. Then if the dice shows three, they must jump forward three places from five, counting as they go… one, two, three. Ask the child to say what number they have landed on, then say the number sentence, 'five add three equals eight'.

Key vocabulary: Number track, numbers to 10, start, count on, jump forward, land on, dice, add, equals.

Extension ideas: Write the number sentence 5 + 3 = 8 on a handheld whiteboard or in chalk on the floor for the children to see.

Activity 6: One more

Type of activity: Adult-led, groups of up to 10 children.

Resources: Climbing wall or low wall.

What to do: Invite one children to climb up on the wall. Say, 'there is one child on the wall'. Invite a second child to climb up and say, 'there is one more child on the wall'. Ask the children what one more than one is.

Say, 'there are two children on the wall'. Ask another child to climb up and say, 'there is one more child on the wall'. Ask the children what one more than two is. Continue until all 10 children are on the wall.

Key vocabulary: Numbers to 10, add, one more, how many?

Extension ideas: Use playground chalk to draw a number track on the floor from zero to 10. Each time a child climbs up onto the wall draw an arc jumping from one number to the next and say, 'one more than... is...'.

Enhancing continuous provision

As already explained, the concept of addition is best introduced through practical activities. Complement adult-led activities by providing resources that the children can use to practise separating and combining during independent play.

Join the children and model using objects and equipment to count, sort, combine and add to. Talk casually about what you are doing as you 'join' sets of objects and work out how many you have 'altogether'. Then as children grow in confidence introduce the use of more formal mathematical language such as 'add', 'sum', 'total' and 'equals'. All the time, challenge the children to copy and extend with their own ideas.

Area of provision	Enhancements that help children to develop an understanding of addition
Water	Provide toy sea creatures, coloured ice cubes, boats and glass pebbles for children to sort into sets, count and combine. Provide tubs, buckets and fishing nets for sorting and combining.
Sand	Provide toy dinosaurs, farm animals and minibeasts, shells, pebbles, treasure and coins for children to sort into sets, count and combine. Provide tubs, buckets and sieves for sorting and combining.
Construction	Provide magnetic bricks for children to make towers they can add to and snakes they can separate into parts. Provide trucks for children to collect and move bricks, sort and add them to piles, walls and structures.
Role Play	Fire engine: Use a cardboard box to make a fire engine with different coloured cardboard wheels attached with velcro that children can remove and replace. Market florist: Provide fake flowers the children can count out, separate into bunches and add to to make bouquets.
Investigation	Hang up a washing line. Provide large laminated number cards, pegs and giant dice. Provide tubs and natural objects for counting, sorting, separating and combining. Provide whiteboards and pens for children to record their thinking about addition.
Physical	Provide a dice and draw large number tracks and a giant snakes and ladders game on the floor. Paint large numbered targets on walls and floors for children to aim balls at and calculate total scores.
Garden	Paint dots onto stepping stones to represent numbers increasing by one each time to 10. Remember to start with a blank for zero.

Curriculum links

Learning about addition covers the following areas of learning and development:

EYFS	Separates a group of three or four objects in different ways, beginning to recognise that the total is still the same; finds the total number of objects in two groups by counting all of them; finds one more from a group of up to 10 objects; begins to use the vocabulary involved in addition; using quantities and objects, adds two single-digit numbers and counts on find the answer.
NIC	Carries out simple mental calculations, for example, 1 more than within 10, 2 more than within 10; understands the concept of addition by combining sets of objects to find 'how many'.
SCE	Uses practical materials and can 'count on' to help understand addition, recording ideas and solutions in different ways; uses addition when solving problems, making best use of the mental strategies and written skills developed.
WFPF	Begins to develop mental calculation strategies during counting and grouping activities, games and through day-to-day classroom activities; progresses from counting on to mental mathematics involving addition with small numbers, using own methods to record calculations.

Subtracting

Understanding that subtraction is the inverse of addition will make it easier for children when it comes to learning calculation strategies later on in their education. Therefore, in the early years it is important to help children begin to develop an understanding of the relationship between addition and subtraction by planning plenty of opportunities to play with both calculation methods.

Subtraction involves the following skills and concepts:

- Being able to count accurately

- Understanding that subtraction involves taking objects away

- Having a secure understanding of number order

- Being able to count back from a given number

- Understanding and being able to use language such as 'subtract', 'take away', 'fewer', 'count back', 'left' and 'total'

- Being able to say the number that is one less than a given number

- Knowing without counting how many there are in sets of up to five objects

- Understanding how to find the 'difference' between two sets of objects.

In the first instance plan opportunities to count back and find one less, as well as taking away objects from a set to find out how many are left. Then practise more difficult skills such as counting up to find how many are missing and comparing sets of objects to find the difference.

Activity 1: Take it away

Type of activity: Adult-led, small groups.

Resources: Grassy area or flower patch, 10 toy magical creatures, magic wand.

What to do: Set up a small world magical scene with 10 magical creatures. Encourage the children to join in and count the creatures and say, 'There are 10 creatures'. Wave the magic wand and say a spell, for example, 'Abracadabra have no fear, I'll wave my wand and you'll disappear!' Pick up two creatures, hide them behind your back and say, 'My wand has magicked two creatures away'. Invite the children to count how many creatures are left then say, 'There are eight creatures left'.

Repeat this activity several times. Each time begin with all 10 creatures and invite children to wave the wand while you chant the spell and take away different numbers of creatures.

Key vocabulary: Numbers to 10, how many? take away, how many left?

Extension ideas: Say the number sentence, '10 take away two is eight'. Write the number sentence $10 - 2 = 8$ on a handheld whiteboard or in chalk on the floor for the children to see.

Add a bit of magic to maths.

Activity 2: Counting back

Type of activity: Adult-led, small groups of four children.

Resources: 25 beans, five small plant pots.

What to do: Give the children a plant pot each and count five beans into each child's hand. Tell them to take away one bean and put in the pot. Say, 'You have one less bean' then help them count how many beans they each have left. Tell them to take away another bean. Say, 'You have one less bean. How many do you have left?' Repeat until there are no beans left.

Key vocabulary: Count, take away, one less, how many left?

Extension ideas: Help the children to visualise what happens to numbers as you count back and they decrease by one each time. Arrange five sets of beans: start with a set of five, then four, three, two and one. Invite the children to count down from five to zero as you point to each set in turn.

Activity 3: Subtracting skittles

Type of activity: Adult-led, small groups.

Resources: Five skittles and a ball.

What to do: Arrange the skittles so they are standing together. Bring the children together and count the skittles to establish that there are five in total. Invite the children to take turns bowling the ball at the skittles to knock over as many as they can. Each time, go over to the skittles and count how many are still standing and ask the children to hold up the corresponding number of fingers. Then encourage them to count up to five, whilst unfurling the remaining fingers.

Repeat until everyone has had a turn.

Key vocabulary: Numbers to five, total, count, how many standing? count up, difference.

Extension ideas: Say the number sentence, 'five take away three is two'. Write $5 - 3 = 2$ on a handheld whiteboard for the children to see.

HOME LINKS

Ask parents to help their children develop an understanding of subtraction by involving them in mathematical conversation when doing outdoor activities. Give examples such as counting how many slices of quiche there are left in a picnic or singing Five Little Ducks when visiting the local pond.

Sing number rhymes such as Five Little Ducks when visiting the real thing.

Activity 5: Five Green and Speckled Frogs

Type of activity: Adult-initiated, during independent play.

Resources: Log, puddle or water tray, five toy frogs.

What to do: Put a log next to a puddle or inside the water tray. Place five toy frogs in a row on the log and invite some children over. Begin by counting the frogs and say, 'There are five frogs on the log'. Then encourage the children to join in the rhyme:

Five green and speckled frogs,
Sat on a speckled log,
Eating the most delicious grubs,
Yum yum.
One jumped into the pool,
Where it was nice and cool…

Pause and pick one frog off the log. Drop it into the water and say, 'There were five frogs on the log. One frog has jumped into the water. How many frogs are left?' Then finish the rhyme:

Then there were just four speckled frogs,
Grub grub.

Repeat the rhyme again, pause and invite a child to pick another frog off the log.

Say, 'Izzy has taken away another frog. How many are left this time?'

Repeat the rhyme again and ask another child to pick one of the remaining frogs off the log. This time say, 'There is one less frog on the log. How many are left now?'

Continue until there are no frogs left on the log.

Key vocabulary: Numbers to five, take away, less, count, how many left?

Extension ideas: Sing the rhyme again but with more frogs. Try the same activity while singing other rhymes including Five Little Monkeys (using a sheet or parachute), Ten Green Bottles (using plastic bottles) and Ten Fat Sausages (on a pretend barbecue).

Activity 4: The count down to Christmas

Type of activity: Adult-led, whole group.

Resources: Enough miniature Christmas gnomes for all the children in the group, tinsel, Christmas lights suitable for outdoors, glitter, permanent marker pen.

What to do: Set up a Christmas garden. Write the children's names under the gnomes in permanent marker then add them to the display.

Time the activity so it starts the correct number of days before the Christmas holidays. For instance, if there are 15 children in the group, start the activity 15 days before the holiday begins.

Bring the children together, count the gnomes and explain there is one each. Explain the gnomes are going to help with the count down to the Christmas holidays.

Each day one gnome will go home with someone until there are none left. Each day take the children outside and choose a gnome. Turn it over, read the name and give it to its new owner. Then count how many gnomes there are left and say, 'There are 10 days left until the holidays'.

Key vocabulary: Count, how many left? take away, countdown.

Extension ideas: Make Advent Calendars with the children so they can do their own countdown to Christmas Day at home.

Don't forget to think about…

…the most difficult subtraction concept for young children to grasp is finding the difference. Plan activities that involve counting the objects in two sets to find out which as the most/least. Help the children find the difference by counting how many more/less there are in each set.

Enhancing continuous provision

Like addition, the concept of subtraction is best introduced through practical games and play. Complement adult-led activities by providing resources that will encourage the children to independently play with subtraction by counting out sets of objects and reducing them in number. Set up games and play scenarios that involve children taking away, counting back and moving backwards. Find suggestions below for toys, resources and games that will encourage children to play in this way.

Join the children as they play and model using objects and equipment to count, sort, remove, reduce and compare. Talk casually about what you are doing as you 'take away' from sets of objects and work out 'how many are left'. Then as they grow in confidence introduce the use of more formal mathematical language such as 'subtract', 'total', 'equals' and 'difference'. All the time, challenge the children to copy and extend with their own ideas.

Area of provision	Enhancements that help children to develop an understanding of subtraction
Water	Provide floats, boats and plastic tubs, together with small items such as toy characters, counters or glass pebbles for children to load and remove. Provide five plastic ducks and some fishing nets for children to sing Five Little Ducks.
Sand	Fill treasure chests and bury them for children to dig up and take the treasure out. Bury 10 rocks and provide dumper trucks for children remove them from the sand.
Construction	Provide building blocks for children to build towers using different numbers of bricks and compare the difference. Build a wall with rubber bricks. Attach some string to a large black foam ball that the children can use as a wrecking ball and knock over the bricks.
Role Play	Train station: Draw a platform on the floor and use banana boxes to make a train so the children can count how many passengers are on board and how many have got off. Rocket: Draw a space rocket on the floor featuring numbers 10 down to zero and write 'BLAST OFF' at the bottom. Make a rocket out of a cardboard box so the children can do their own countdown and take off.
Investigation	Give the children a giant dice and thread 10 airflow balls onto a rope and tie it up for the children to use as an abacus. Provide whiteboards and pens for children to record their thinking about subtraction.
Physical	Provide a dice and draw large number tracks and a giant snakes and ladders game on the floor. Set up games of skittles, line up plastic bottles or cans for children to knock down, count how many have fallen and how many are left.
Garden	Place sets of 10 garden ornaments around such as gnomes, toadstools and windmills for children to practise counting and taking away.

Curriculum links

Learning about subtraction covers the following areas of learning and development:

EYFS	Finds one less from a group of up to 10 objects; begins to use the vocabulary involved in subtraction; using quantities and objects, subtracts two single-digit numbers and counts on or back to find the answer.
NIC	Carries out simple mental calculations, for example, 1 less than within 10, 2 less than within 10; investigates the relationship between addition and subtraction in practical situations.
SCE	Uses practical materials and can 'count on and back' to help understand subtraction, recording ideas and solutions in different ways; uses subtraction when solving problems, making best use of the mental strategies and written skills developed.
WFPF	Begins to develop mental calculation strategies during counting and grouping activities, games and through day-to-day classroom activities; begins to understand the relationship between addition and subtraction.

Multiplying and dividing

Like addition and subtraction, multiplication and division come hand in hand as the inversion of each other. Multiplication can be described as counting in groups and division as sharing out or dividing equally. A firm understanding of both begins with early exploration of number patterns and sequences through practical activities and everyday observations.

Multiplying and dividing involve the following skills and concepts:

- Being able to count accurately

- Knowing without counting how many there are in sets of up to five objects

- Understanding that multiplication involves combining sets of equal amounts

- Understanding that division involves sharing into sets of equal amounts

- Understanding and being able to use language such as 'double', 'group', 'pair', 'halve', 'share' and 'divide'.

In the first instance practitioners should plan opportunities to practise multiplication by counting in twos through activities involving pairing objects. Children are introduced to sorting and grouping objects into sets, then adding the total number of sets together. Division at this stage involves halving, as well as sharing out and dividing sets of objects into groups.

The need for practical early exploration of the concepts that underpin calculation makes this aspect of mathematics particularly suited to outdoor learning, where children can experience physically adding, subtracting, multiplying and dividing.

Activity 1: Pair them up

Type of activity: Adult-initiated, during independent play.

Resources: Washing line or string, five pairs of socks or gloves or same coloured/patterned T-shirts, washing basket, pegs.

What to do: Tie up a washing line and fill a basket with matching pairs of socks. Invite children to come to the line and help you match and hang them in pairs. Ask the children how many socks are on the line altogether. Once they have counted, explain there is a quicker way to find out – by counting in twos. Point out the socks are arranged in pairs of two. Demonstrate counting the socks in twos. Repeat and encourage the children to join in.

Key vocabulary: Numbers to 10, how many? match, pair, count in twos, altogether, total.

Extension ideas: Introduce laminated number cards and peg them next to the pairs to show the number sequence 2, 4, 6, 8, 10. Increase the number of clothing items to 20.

Use a washing line to introduce the concept of doubling.

Activity 3: Teddy bears' picnic

Type of activity: Adult-led, small groups.

Resources: Five teddy bears, five plates, five bowls, five cups, five sets of cutlery, picnic basket, picnic blanket.

What to do: Set up a teddy bears' picnic. Lay out a blanket and five teddy bears on it in a circle. Invite the children help share out sets of plates, bowls, cups, forks, knives and spoons. Introduce some toy foods that can be shared out and divided, for example sliced pizza, bunches of grapes and pieces of cake.

All the time talk about what the children are doing and model mathematical language associated with division. For example, ask them to 'share out' the plates and ensure the bears have 'one each'. Count how many bears there are and ask the children how many spoons they need to ensure they all have the 'same'. Ask them to 'divide up' the pizza and 'share' it out. Challenge them to 'share out' the grapes so that all the bears have the 'same'.

Key vocabulary: How many? divide, share, equal, same, count, check.

Extension ideas: Give the children other items to share out but do not give them enough. Ask them to work out how many more they need to ensure all the bears have their fair share.

Activity 2: Half each

Type of activity: Adult-led, small even numbered groups.

Resources: Ready prepared sandwiches, Mini Babybel cheeses, mini pizzas, fairy cakes, paper plates, blunt plastic knives.

What to do: Divide the children into small even numbered groups and assign an adult to each. Ask the children to divide themselves into pairs. Give each adult a plate of picnic foods that can be divided in half. Ask the adults to give each pair of children a knife and two plates. Then give one child in each pair a piece of food that can be cut in half, for example a sandwich or Mini Babybel cheese. The child must then cut the food and give their partner half. Repeat with different foods, ensuring all children get a chance to divide something in half.

Key vocabulary: Share, halve, divide, half.

Extension ideas: Give the children small, even amounts of grapes, raisins or cherry tomatoes to help them understand that halving involves dividing into two equal shares.

HOME LINKS

Ask parents to help their children develop an understanding of multiplication and division by involving them in outdoor tasks that involve calculation. Give examples such as sharing out plant pots, dividing up seeds for planting, pairing up laundry items for the line and sweeping up half of the leaves.

Create a visual representation of counting in multiples.

Activity 4: Tower building on the double

Type of activity: Adult-initiated, with individuals during independent play.

Resources: Building blocks, number cards one to five.

What to do: Set out a pile of bricks and invite a child over. Ask her to pick a card and say the number. Invite her to select the corresponding number of bricks and build a tower. Explain you would like to make the tower twice as high and this means doubling the number of bricks. Help the child pick the same number of bricks again and add them to the tower to make it twice as high. Count the total number of bricks and say, 'We started with a tower of four bricks and doubled them to make a tower of eight. Double four is eight'. Knock the tower down and start again.

Key vocabulary: Numbers to 10, double, total, count, how many?

Extension ideas: Build a series of towers in a row, each double the height of the one before.

Activity 5: Pebble pattern multiplication

Type of activity: Adult-led, small groups.

Resources: Large space, plentiful supply of similar sized pebbles, playground chalk.

What to do: Draw a number line on the floor or wall. Explain you are going to use the number line to count in multiples of two. Use a piece of chalk to draw a jump from zero to two and then on to four, six, eight and 10. Go back to the beginning, point to the numbers and repeat the count.

Invite the children to help you count out enough pebbles to make a visual representation. Start with placing two pebbles in a column. Then place a column of four next to it and another column of six next to that. Continue with columns of eight and 10.

Take time to look at the pattern. Point to each column as you count in twos. Underline the multiples of two as you do so. Point out that each column has two more pebbles than the last.

Key vocabulary: Count in twos, number pattern, multiple.

Extension ideas: Repeat but create columns representing multiples of five.

Activity 6: Equal shares

Type of activity: Adult-led, small groups.

Resources: Plant pots, daffodil bulbs, compost, gardening tools.

What to do: Give each child three plant pots and six daffodil bulbs. Explain you would like them to 'divide' the bulbs 'equally' between the plant pots so each pot has the 'same' number of bulbs in it.

Invite the children to fill their pots with compost. Then ask them to place an equal number of bulbs on top of the compost in each pot. Encourage them to 'share out' the bulbs one at a time until there are two bulbs sitting on top of each pot.

Pause to count how many pots there are. Then count how many bulbs are in total. Then count how many bulbs there are on each pot. Say the number sentence, 'six shared between three is two'. Invite the children to bury their bulbs in the compost.

Key vocabulary: Share, divide, equal.

Extension ideas: Play around with different numbers of plant pots and bulbs.

Enhancing continuous provision

Enhance the outdoor learning environment to encourage children to play with concepts surrounding multiplication and division. Provide resources that prompt children to count, sort, divide, share group, pair and create number patterns naturally as they play. Set up games and activities that involve children dividing and grouping themselves.

Join the children as they play and model using objects and equipment to count, group and share. Talk casually about what you are doing as you 'share out' resources and 'pair up' toys. As children grow in confidence use more formal mathematical language such as 'multiply', 'divide', 'total' and 'equals'.

Area of provision	Enhancements that help children to develop an understanding of multiplication and division
Water	Provide sets of equally sized bottles, cups and containers for children to fill, sort and group. Place different coloured frozen jelly cubes in cold water for the children to sort, group and share.
Sand	Provide pairs of coloured buckets and equal sets of coloured tubs for children to arrange in pairs and sort into groups. Bury equal sets of sorting objects for children to dig up and group.
Construction	Provide pairs of tools and sets of coloured and shaped bricks that can be divided and grouped. Put out pairs of toy trucks, bulldozers, steam rollers and diggers.
Role Play	Pizza shack: Provide decorated paper plates cut into slices for the children to divide between themselves. River boat cruises: Use banana boxes to make a pair of boats that children can divide themselves between. Make more boats so children can create more groups of passengers.
Investigation	Provide a bucket of pebbles for children to count, sort, group and create patterns. Start a number pattern made of conkers, stones or pebbles and write in chalk on the ground next to it. Can you continue the number pattern?
Physical	Paint or draw number snakes and number squares on the floor and walls with multiples of two, five and 10 highlighted in different colours. Provide pairs and sets of balls, skittles, beanbags, quoits, baskets and tubs for children to sort, group and share.
Garden	Provide pairs of gardening gloves, sets of coloured plant pots and identical sets of gardening tools. Provide seed boxes containing large seeds that can be sorted, grouped and divided.

Curriculum links

Learning about multiplication and division covers the following areas of learning and development:

EYFS	Separates a group of three or four objects in different ways, beginning to recognise that the total is still the same; solves problems, including doubling, halving and sharing.
NIC	Investigates different ways of partitioning sets into subsets practically, talks abut the outcomes; explores pattern in number; extends activities to include counting in 2s, 5s and 10s.
SCE	Explores numbers and uses them to create sequences; uses multiplication and division when solving problems, making best use of the mental strategies and written skills developed.
WFPF	Begins to understand the relationship between multiplication and division, halving and doubling; recognises and investigates patterns, sequences and relationships.

Problem solving

Problem solving activities are absolutely essential in the early years because they present practitioners with the opportunity to foster sustained shared thinking by opening up discussion and debate that encourages children to talk about their thoughts and ideas. The very nature of mathematics makes it an ideal subject for practising problem solving skills.

Mathematical problem solving involves the following skills and concepts:

- Being able to count accurately

- Understanding and being able to use basic calculation strategies

- Being able to identify what type of mathematical knowledge is needed to solve the problem

- Being able to organise and process information

- Being able to think logically, identify patterns and make links

- Being able to verbalise thoughts, make predictions and explain ideas

- Being able to weigh up and find solutions.

Problem solving makes maths relevant because it gives children a reason to use it. What's more, it helps children develop metacognitive knowledge (thinking about their own thinking). When children are asked to explain their ideas, reflect upon and evaluate their thoughts, they begin to gain an understanding of their own thought processes. This is all part of being a creative and critical thinker.

Activity 1: Car wash

Type of activity: Adult-led, small groups.

Resources: Buckets, sponges, shammies, soapy water, cars, trikes.

What to do: Invite six children to help clean three play vehicles. Ask the children to divide themselves into pairs and then allocate them a vehicle. Provide four buckets, six sponges and three shammies and instruct all six children to come and select from the equipment. Explain each pair will need one bucket, one sponge and one shammy. Help the children divide up the equipment with prompts and questions such as, 'Are there enough buckets for one each?', 'What else do you need?' and 'How many sponges and shammies do you need between you?'.

Key vocabulary: Count, how many? share, divide, each, pair, enough, too many.

Extension ideas: Add another vehicle. Look at the left over equipment and ask the children if there are enough buckets, sponges and shammies for another pair of children to come over and join in.

Find number problems in small world play.

Activity 2: Animal escape!

Type of activity: Adult-initiated, during independent play.

Resources: Small world wild animals, something to represent animal enclosures (small shoe box lids or margarine containers) lined with straw, wood shavings or soil, number cards.

What to do: Set up a zoo outside amongst some shrubbery, a flower patch or rocky patch. Make five animal enclosures of roughly equal size. Scatter some toy wild animals amongst the shrubs, flowers and rocks. You will need one giraffe, two elephants, three monkeys, four lions and five tigers (or a variation of the same). Invite some children over and explain that all the animals have escaped from the zoo. Challenge them to find them and put them back in their enclosures. Explain they will need to sort and match the animals so they are in enclosures together. When the children have finished, ask them to count how many there are of each animal. Talk about the difference between the numbers of animals in the enclosures. Challenge the children to arrange the enclosures in numerical order and match number cards to each.

Key vocabulary: Numbers to five, how many? count, check, order, one more, one less.

Extension ideas: Change the numbers of animals so that the number in each set increases by two and explore number pattern.

Activity 3: Build it

Type of activity: Adult-initiated, during independent play.

Resources: 'Build it' construction kit (or other large construction that involves using nuts and bolts), digital camera, laminator.

What to do: Build three different simple models using the 'Build it' construction kit. Take a photo of each model and laminate it for the children to look at and copy. Set out the construction kit in sets of pieces that match the laminated pictures. Take away some nuts and bolts from each set and put them into a tub of spares. Invite children over to build the models. When they get stuck, ask them to work out how many of each piece is missing, then indicate them towards the tub of spares to select what they need.

Key vocabulary: How many are missing? count, how many more? enough, too many.

Extension ideas: Complicate the problem. Give one child too many pieces and another not enough so they have to discuss what they each have and work out who needs what.

Make maths relevant.

Activity 5: An even spread

Type of activity: Adult-led, small groups.

Resources: Large planters or plant pots, different coloured flowers, compost, gardening tools.

What to do: Bring three large planters into the setting. Explain you would like to evenly space them around the outdoor area and ask the children to help decide where to put them. Prompt with observations like, 'Those two look quite close together' and 'I wonder what will happen if we put it there'. Once the planters are in place get the children to help fill them with compost. Then bring out three different types of flower for planting, for example, yellow magnolias, red primroses and purple pansies. Explain you would like to evenly spread the colours between the planters and need some help to decide where to plant them. Help the children tackle the problem with question prompts such as, 'What do you think we should do first?', 'How can we make sure the flowers are spread evenly between the planters?' and 'How do you think that looks?' At first just place the plants on top of the soil so the children can reflect upon their decisions and change their minds. When they are happy with the arrangement help them plant the flowers.

Key vocabulary: How many? where? count, enough, not enough, change, different, decide, even, divide, colour, arrange.

Extension ideas: Increase the number of flowers or colours.

Don't forget to think about...

...motivating the children by making maths relevant to them. Present problems that are meaningful and based around the children's interests. As well as setting up and presenting children with problems, be on the look out for spontaneous problem solving opportunities that arise during the children's self directed activities.

Activity 4: Missing minibeasts

Type of activity: Adult-led, small groups.

Resources: 10 toy minibeasts.

What to do: Create a small world minibeast setting in a flowerbed or large plant pot amongst the plants and flowers. Use a total of 10 minibeasts that are easy to see and count. Invite some children to look at the scene and count how many minibeasts there are altogether. Tell the children to turn around so they cannot see. Take away two minibeasts and ask the children to have a look and work out how many are missing. Prompt the children with questions such as, 'How many minibeasts were there at the start?', 'How many minibeasts are left?' and 'What do you need to do to work out how many are missing?' Show the children how to work it out using their fingers. Ask them to hold up 10 fingers, then fold down one at a time as you all count back to eight.

Key vocabulary: Count, take away, how many? altogether, count back, difference.

Extension ideas: Introduce the counting up method. Start at eight and count up to 10 with your fingers to show that the difference is two.

Look for opportunities to present children with mathematical problems as they play.

Enhancing continuous provision

Encourage children to use thinking skills when outside by presenting them with mathematical problems to solve. Display question ideas, challenges and discussion points that practitioners can refer to when joining play. This can be done on laminated cards, easels, flip charts or even in chalk on the floor or walls. Below are suggestions for key questions that aim to prompt discussion, as well as comments that aim to support, develop and extend thinking.

Area of provision	Enhancements that help children to practise problem solving
Water	Float a set of boats, put glass pebbles in the water and set a challenge to: Fill all the boats with the same number of pebbles. Helpful questions/comments include: Crikey! That's so full it's overflowing, I'm not sure that's very fair and How can you check if they all have the same amount?
Sand	Create a small world treasure island with a wrecked ship and some pirates. Bury a small chest of coins and set a challenge to: Discover the treasure and give everyone their fair share. Helpful questions/comments include: There doesn't seem to be much treasure, He looks like he's got a lot and How do you know it is fair?
Construction	Paint numbers to 20 on building blocks. Remove some and ask: Which numbers are missing? Helpful questions/comments include: What number comes before/after? And Those blocks are in a right jumble aren't they?
Role Play	Set up a campsite and set a challenge to: Make a tent with enough room to fit two people. Helpful questions/comments include: What do you think you will need? That's a small blanket and look at all that space!
Investigation	Lay out some pebbles and set a challenge to: Continue the number pattern. Helpful questions/comments include: How many more pebbles are there in the second column than the first? and Look at how pebbles are arranged like steps.
Physical	Put out a sand timer and some skipping ropes and set a challenge: How many skips/jumps/hops can you do in one minute? or Which can you do the most of in one minute – hops, skips or jumps?
Garden	Set the challenge: Which is the most popular spot for snails? Helpful questions/comments include: I can't seem to find any snails here? and How do you know they like it there so much?

Curriculum links

Mathematical problem solving covers the following areas of learning and development:

EYFS	Begins to identify own mathematical problems based on own interests and fascinations; shows an interest in and solves problems.
NIC	Explores number; is involved in solving practical problems.
SCE	Understands the application of mathematics; applies skills and understanding creatively and logically to solve problems within a variety of contexts.
WFPF	Selects and uses appropriate mathematical ideas, equipment and materials to solve practical problems; identifies, collects and organises information in purposeful contexts; develops a variety of mathematical approaches and strategies.

Shape

Exploration of shape is important in the early years because it helps children develop a sense of how our world is constructed. Exploring the properties of shape teaches children about form and function, which is applicable to science, design and technology.

Knowledge of shape is underpinned by the following skills and concepts:

- Being able to name shapes

- Understanding that a 2D shape is flat

- Understanding that a 3D shape is solid

- Being able to recognise and describe shapes in the environment and talk about form in relation to purpose

- Understanding and being able to use language such as 'side', 'corner', 'round', 'edge', 'flat', 'face' and 'solid'

- Understanding that two shapes with the same properties are the same, even if one is in a different position.

Children learn about the properties of shape through practical exploration of both two and three dimensional objects. They need opportunities to create pictures and patterns, construct models and play games with shapes. They also need to be set challenges and tasks that require them to select specific shapes for particular purposes.

The following activities take advantage of the outdoor environment for providing resources that children can explore and examine to learn more about shape and space in relation to form, function and purpose.

Activity 1: Shape hunt

Type of activity: Adult-led, small groups.

Resources: Child-friendly digital cameras.

What to do: Go outside and look around at shapes in the built environment. Point out bricks in buildings, windows and windowpanes, roofs, stepping stones, doors, fence panels, wire fencing and buildings. Encourage children to describe and name the shapes they see.

Give the children cameras so they can take photographs of the different shaped objects. Print and laminate the pictures and create an indoor display of shapes in the environment.

Key vocabulary: Shape, side, long, round, corner, edge, length, purpose, reason, square, cube, circle, sphere, triangle, triangular prism, rectangle, cuboid.

Extension ideas: Look at how objects are designed to fit together, for example, the bricks in a wall, panes of glass in a window and tiles on a roof. Talk about the purpose of shape, for example the triangular roofs that encourage rainwater to run off and cuboid buildings designed to fit together to make the best use of space.

Look for shapes in nature and the built environment.

Activity 2: Shapes in nature

Type of activity: Adult-led, small groups.

Resources: Baskets for collecting objects.

What to do: Send the children to collect a range of natural objects. When they come back look at what they have found and examine each object's shape and form. Engage the children in discussion about natural design and purpose. For example:

Leaves: Flat to catch sunlight and take in carbon dioxide, which is essential for photosynthesis.

Conkers and acorns: Round so they roll easily, spread out and grow into new plants.

Sycamore seeds: Flat propeller so they float on the breeze, spread out and grow into new plants.

Chestnuts: Spiky shells for protection against hungry animals.

Twigs: Long and thin to help spread out leaves so they can catch the sunlight.

Key vocabulary: Shape, round, flat, long, thin, spike, purpose, reason, spherical.

Extension ideas: Show the children a picture of the interior of a beehive. Explain the cells are shaped like hexagons so they fit tightly together without leaving gaps, a good use of space. Collect hailstones and use a magnifier to look at the shapes of the individual pieces.

Activity 3: Large-scale shape printing

Type of activity: Adult-led, small groups.

Resources: Large roll of paper, poster paints, large containers (shallow ice cream tubs), example 2D shapes, warm soapy water, towel.

What to do: Roll out some large pieces of paper and squirt different coloured paints into large containers. Invite the children to dip their feet in the paints and walk on the paper to create shapes. Talk to each child before they start and ask what shape they are going to make. Ask them to describe what the shape looks like, how many sides it has and how many corners. If need be refer to an example. Get them to print one edge at a time, pause to dip their feet back in the paint and think about where they are going to move next.

Key vocabulary: Shape, how many sides/corners? edge, side, corner, straight, curved, round, long, short, equal, square, circle, rectangle, triangle, two dimensional.

Extension ideas: Cut out the shapes once dry and ask the children to arrange them into pictures, for example, a square and triangle to make a house.

Sculpt shapes out of snow.

Activity 4: Body shapes

Type of activity: Adult-led, small groups of no less than six.

Resources: Digital camera, plastic 2D shapes (square, circle, triangle, rectangle), bag.

What to do: Tell the children they are going to make some giant 2D shapes using their bodies. Choose a child to pick a shape out of the bag and name it. Ask the children to describe the features of the shape. If it is a square, for example, they should point out the four corners and four equal sides. Help the children form the shape on the floor using their bodies. A square would require four children, a rectangle six and a triangle three. Each time the children make a shape take a photo and show it to them so they can see how it looks.

Key vocabulary: Shape, two dimensional, flat, side, edge, corner, length, long, short, equal, square, circle, triangle, rectangle, how many sides/corners?

Extension ideas: Make more complex shapes such as a hexagon and oval.

Activity 5: Snow structures

Type of activity: Adult-initiated, during independent play.

Resources: Different shaped containers, spades.

What to do: Challenge the children to build with snow. Show them how to pack snow into containers, tip them out and create bricks. Make big and small bricks using buckets, ice cream tubs, plant pots and plastic pudding bowls. Attempt to make a small igloo and talk about which shaped bricks are easiest to build with. Roll the snow into big round balls and build snow people.

Key vocabulary: Shape, cube, cuboid, cone, round, flat, solid, surface, sphere, fit, gap, mould, three dimensional.

Extension ideas: Provide a variety of different shaped containers for children to fill with snow and create different 3D shaped snow moulds.

Activity 6: 3D castle construction

Type of activity: Adult-initiated, during independent play.

Resources: Laminated pictures of castles, boxes, crates, large building blocks, (including cylindrical, cone, pyramid and triangular prism shapes).

What to do: Look at some pictures of real castles and talk about the shapes and features in the architecture. Point out rounded doors, thin rectangular windows, blocky battlements and cone shaped turret roofs. Challenge the children to build a castle using large construction equipment. As they build, name the shapes they are using and talk about their properties. Ask the children to explain why they have chosen certain shapes of block for particular purposes.

Key vocabulary: Shape, three dimensional, cube, cuboid, cone, cylinder, triangular prism, square, rectangle, round, triangle, curved, narrow, wide, edge, face.

Extension ideas: Dismantle some cardboard boxes and flatten them out. Look at the 2D shapes that each box is made of. Build the boxes back up into their 3D shapes, stick them with tape and point out the 2D shapes again.

Build with 3D shapes to find out about space, form and function.

Enhancing continuous provision

Encourage children to examine and explore shapes during independent play by providing a range of resources that they can build, model and construct with. Set up activities that require them to take account of the properties of different shapes, as well as resources that prompt them to use shape and form creatively.

Join the children as they play and talk about the shapes they are using. Model the use of mathematical language to name and describe the shapes and their properties.

Area of provision	Enhancements that help children to develop an understanding of shape
Water	Provide plastic shapes and fishing nets. Freeze different shaped ice cubes with added food colouring. Put small 3D shapes inside balloons, fill them with water, freeze them and put them in the water tray to gradually melt and reveal the shapes.
Sand	Provide variously shaped sand moulds and spades. Fill the sand tray with a variety of different dry pasta shapes (buy coloured pasta or dye it with food colouring). Mix damp sand with PVA glue and leave it to set in ice cube trays to create sand bricks.
Construction	Provide different shaped plastic plant pots, seed trays, boxes, containers, kitchen rolls, strong tape, string and wire for the children to do some outdoor junk modelling. Provide plastic containers for children to fill with mud and make bricks. Set out large building blocks, Giant Polydron and real bricks.
Role Play	Freelance photographers: Provide child-friendly digital cameras and employ children to take photos of shapes in the outdoor environment.
Investigation	Set up an investigation that involves rolling different shaped objects down a ramp. Display a challenge card that reads Find out which shaped objects travel down the easiest. Set up an easel or provide clipboards for the children to record their results. Challenge the children to collect natural objects and use them to create pictures and collages.
Physical	Provide playground chalks and set up easels for children to draw and paint shapes. Provide large cardboard boxes for children to build with, climb inside and open up. Provide inset jigsaws and giant puzzles.
Garden	Put out some baskets labelled with laminated pictures of a cube/square, sphere/circle, pyramid/triangle and cuboid/rectangle. Put some objects from the outdoor area in the baskets to encourage children to start collections of different shaped outdoor and natural objects.

Curriculum links

Learning about shape covers the following areas of learning and development:

EYFS	Shows interest in shape by sustained construction activity or by talking about shapes or arrangements; shows interest in shapes in the environment; uses shapes appropriately for tasks; explores characteristics of everyday objects, 'solid' 3D shapes and 'flat' 2D shapes and uses mathematical language to describe them.
NIC	Explores and talks about shapes in the environment; describes, names, builds and makes models with 3D shapes and pictures and patterns with 2D shapes; investigates and talks about properties of shapes using appropriate mathematical language.
SCE	Enjoys investigating objects and shapes and can sort, describe and be creative with them; explores simple 3D objects and 2D shapes and can identify, name and describe their features using appropriate vocabulary; can explore and discuss how and why different shapes fit together.
WFPF	Recognises shapes in the environment; understands and uses the properties of shapes: recognises similarities and differences of 2-D and 3-D shapes; knows the names of common 3-D and 2-D shapes; makes increasingly more complex or accurate models and patterns of shapes; sorts shapes according to one or more criteria.

Pattern

Understanding pattern is useful because it is underpinned by the knowledge and use of mathematical conventions. Copying, continuing and creating patterns gives children practical experience of playing with sequences and applying mathematical rules.

Knowledge of pattern is underpinned by the following skills and concepts:

- Being able to differentiate between colours, shapes and size

- Understanding that a pattern repeats

- Being able to identify a sequence and predict how a pattern will continue

- Being able to make up a mathematical rule to create a pattern

- Understanding that something is symmetrical if it is made up of exactly similar parts facing each other

- Understanding and being able to use language such as 'pattern', 'match', 'last', 'next', repeat', 'continue' and 'symmetrical'.

Children learn about pattern through practical experience of copying and continuing patterns created by others.

The outdoor environment is full of natural patterns for children to study and replicate. What's more, nature provides an abundance of resources for children to use to create their own repeating patterns. The following activities take full advantage of these natural resources and make the most of outdoor space with ideas for creating patterns on a large scale.

Activity 1: Natural colour mural

Type of activity: Adult-led, small groups.

Resources: Liquid watercolour paints, trigger spray bottles, large roll of paper, painting aprons or coveralls, baskets for collecting objects.

What to do: Roll out a large piece of paper on the floor and place rocks on the corners to hold it down. Fill some trigger spray bottles with various liquid watercolour paints in different shades of colour. Send the children to collect natural objects such as leaves, grasses and flowers. When they return examine the objects and talk about the colours. Compare lighter and darker shades, such as dark/light green leaves and dark/light yellow flowers.

Ask each child to choose an object and select a matching shade of watercolour spray. Instruct them to place their object on the paper and spray over it, then remove the object to reveal an empty silhouette of its shape. Cover the entire piece of paper. Compare the different shades of colour. Study the shapes of the silhouettes and look for patterns and symmetry.

Key vocabulary: Colour, green, yellow, red, orange, brown, dark, light, match, different, same, pattern, symmetrical.

Extension ideas: Arrange the objects so they create silhouette patterns.

Use natural objects to create repeating patterns.

Activity 3: Paint splat patterns

Type of activity: Adult-led, small groups.

Resources: Painting aprons, poster paints, ice cream tubs, large roll of paper, sponges or beanbags.

What to do: Roll out a large piece of paper on the floor and place rocks on the corners to hold it down. Explain the children are going to dip sponges in different coloured paints and throw them at the paper to create a repeating pattern. Each time a child approaches the paper, pause and ask them to talk through the pattern so far. Help by asking, 'What colours have already been used?', 'What was the last colour?', 'What should come next?', 'Can you describe the pattern so far?'.

Key vocabulary: Repeating pattern, same, different, next, last, every other.

Extension ideas: Make more complex patterns. Take photographs of the patterns created, laminate them and create a book to hang from an outdoor painting easel for children to flick through.

Activity 2: Nature patterns

Type of activity: Adult-initiated, during independent play.

Resources: Baskets for collecting objects, conkers, acorns, sycamore seeds, different coloured leaves, twigs, stones, pebbles, flowers.

What to do: Invite children to collect natural objects and arrange them into repeating patterns. As the children create their patterns talk to them about what they are doing. Ask what came last in the pattern and what they need next. Point to an object and ask them to point to all the others that are the same. Help them make more complex patterns.

Key vocabulary: Repeating pattern, same, different, next, last, every other.

Extension ideas: Challenge children to make patterns with the same objects but based around appearance or texture. For example, a pattern of leaves that are large and small or a pattern of stones that alternates rough and smooth.

Try...

...taking photos of the patterns the children create. Laminate them and display them next to the areas of provision they were created. This will inspire other children to create their own.

Use fabric to weave patterns around railings.

Activity 4: Pattern mobiles

Type of activity: Adult-initiated, during independent play.

Resources: Plastic coat hangers, coloured jewel beads, nylon beading cord.

What to do: Invite children to create repeating patterns using colourful jewel beads. Allow them to create their patterns using a range of criteria, for example, based on shape, colour or size. Once the children have threaded their beads onto beading cord ask them to explain their patterns to you. Talk about the patterns and model the use of mathematical language such as 'You chose to alternate green and blue', 'Your pattern starts with a cube shaped bead and continues with two round beads' and 'I can see you chose to make every other bead small.' Tie the bead patterns to plastic coat hangers and fix them securely outside so they sparkle in the sun.

Key vocabulary: Repeating pattern, every other, shape, colour, size.

Extension ideas: Use old CDs and invite children to print patterns on them in acrylic paint. Then attach them to the bottom of the beads.

Activity 5: Body patterns

Type of activity: Adult-led, large groups of 10.

Resources: Digital camera.

What to do: Begin with experimenting with making body shapes. Ask the children to spread out, watch you and copy your body shape. Practise standing in a star shape, standing tall, stretching up to the sky and crouching into a ball.

Help the children to arrange themselves in a line, standing next to each other but slightly spread apart. Explain they are going to make a simple repeating pattern. Ask the first child in the line to make a shape and hold it. Ask the next child to make a different shape. Take a photo and show it to the third child. Explain the pattern needs to repeat and ask what shape he needs to make next. Once the third child is in shape, take another photo and show it to the forth child. Talk about the last shape in the pattern and what shape comes next. Continue until the pattern is complete.

Take a photo of the complete pattern, print and display it.

Key vocabulary: Repeating pattern, same, different, next, last, every other.

Extension ideas: Make more complex patterns. Display photos of the patterns inside windows facing out for children to copy and recreate.

Activity 6: Natural symmetry

Type of activity: Adult-initiated, during independent play.

Resources: Small hand-held plastic mirrors, child-friendly digital cameras.

What to do: Collect natural objects such as leaves, flower heads and pinecones. Provide mirrors for the children to hold across their centres to reveal their symmetry.

Take a selection of fruits outside. Begin by examining the external appearance before cutting them open to reveal their internal symmetry also.

If possible, take photos of butterflies with their wings open. Print the pictures and study their symmetrical appearance. Provide mirrors for the children to investigate as above.

Key vocabulary: Symmetrical, reflection, facing, similar, opposite.

Extension ideas: Paint symmetrical butterflies. Provide folded sugar paper and ask the children to paint half a butterfly. Fold the paper over and press firmly together.

Enhancing continuous provision

As already mentioned, the outside environment is full of natural resources that lend themselves well to the exploration of pattern. However, it is a good idea to further enhance the outdoor learning area by providing resources and materials that will inspire children to create patterns as they play.

Talk with the children and point out patterns in the natural and built environment. Ask them if they can describe what they see. Prompt them to talk about the shapes in patterns, look at how they are arranged and fit together.

Show an interest in the patterns the children create. Ask them to describe what they have done and challenge them to attempt more complex designs.

Area of provision	Enhancements that encourage children to copy, continue and create patterns
Water	Provide foam shapes for children to arrange into floating patterns. Provide patterned objects, for example, spotty cups, striped fish and patterned sponges for children to play with. Provide pipettes and small bottles of coloured oils for children to drop onto the surface of the water.
Sand	Provide buttons, shells, plastic sorting bugs and animals for children to make repeating patterns. Replace the sand with uncooked pasta or dried beans in a variety of shapes and colours.
Construction	Provide laminated cards showing photos of buildings and structures featuring construction materials that form patterns for the children to study, for example a brick wall, the Shard and the Eiffel Tower. Use playground chalk to write a challenge, for example, Use the bricks to create your own repeating pattern.
Role Play	Set up a market stall that sells patterned fashions: Provide clothing with repeating striped, spotted and floral patterns. Add patterned beaded jewellery.
Investigation	Provide instruments for children to create musical patterns. Display prompt cards with pictorial representations of patterns, for example, a repeating sequence of pictures; drum, triangle, drum, triangle, drum, triangle. Provide freshly cut logs and magnifiers for children to study the patterns of rings in a cross section of a tree trunk.
Physical	Crush playground chalk and mix it with water to make paint for children to paint patterns on the floor and walls. Provide strips of fabric and ribbon for children to create woven patterns around railings and fences.
Garden	Make clay ladybirds, paint them with symmetrical spot patterns and waterproof them with varnish. Place ornamental garden butterflies on sticks in and around the plants. Arrange and plant flowers in patterns.

Curriculum links

Learning about pattern covers the following areas of learning and development:

EYFS	Recognises, creates and describes patterns.
NIC	Investigates and talks about pattern in the environment; copies, creates and continues simple patterns.
SCE	Spots and explores patterns in own and wider environment and copies and continues these to create own patterns.
WFPF	Recognises patterns, sequences and relationships through practical activities and discussion; investigates repeating patterns and relationships to make simple predictions.

Space

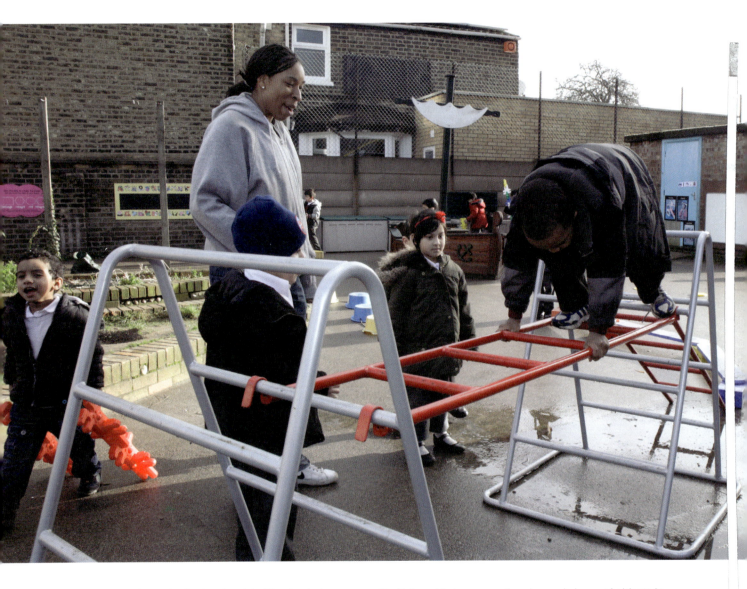

This aspect of mathematics is closely related to physical development and is underpinned by knowledge of position, movement and direction. Having a sense of space gives children independence, confidence and self-control. If children have spacial awareness they are more able to share space with others and manage risk in terms of choosing routes and negotiating obstacles.

Knowledge of space is underpinned by the following skills and concepts:

- Being able to describe the relative position of something or someone

- Being able to describe a route

- Being able to negotiate space and move around obstacles

- Being able to assess the size and shape of objects in terms of their use for a specific purpose

- Being able to arrange and position objects

- Being able to coordinate bodily movements

- Understanding and being able to use positional and directional language.

Children learn about position, moment and direction through play and games that require them to physically negotiate space, coordinate bodily movement, give directions, follow instructions and move and arrange equipment and objects. Of course there is nowhere better suited for these types of activities than outside in the open.

Activity 1: Den building

Type of activity: Adult-initiated, during independent play.

Resources: Sheets, blankets, pegs, clothes horses, chairs, easels, rope, blocks, cardboard boxes, tarpaulin, wide masking tape.

What to do: Challenge the children to build a den. Stand back and look at the available equipment. Look at the size and shape of individual pieces and help the children to consider what they could use for different purposes.

As the children build, help them move and place equipment safely and securely. Encourage them to talk about what they are doing and model the use of mathematical language to describe the relative positioning of the building materials.

Key vocabulary: Next to, in front of, beside, above, size, space, big, small, inside, outside, position, high, low.

Extension ideas: After the children have had a chance to play in the den, ask them if they have any ideas about how it might be improved.

Explore shape and space by building on a large scale.

HOME LINKS

Ask parents to help their children make a map of their journey to the setting. Ask them to write notes on the map using directional language, and give examples such as, 'We walk towards the shop and turn right at the corner' and 'We follow the footpath beside the canal'.

Activity 3: Obstacle course

Type of activity: Adult-initiated, during independent play.

Resources: Tunnels, benches, mats, crates, small trampolines, stepping stones, tyres.

What to do: Set up an obstacle course. Allow the children space to negotiate the obstacles and talk to each other about what they are doing. When the children finish the course ask them to describe how they travelled across it. Elaborate on their remarks by adding description in mathematical language.

Key vocabulary: Along, forward, across, back, under, over, behind, in front, route, start, end, through, inside.

Extension ideas: Help the children rearrange the obstacles. Model the use of positional language to describe the new layout.

Activity 2: Follow the leader

Type of activity: Adult-initiated, during independent play.

Resources: Large outdoor space.

What to do: Start a game of follow the leader. Invite children to follow you around in a large space, copying your movements and following your direction. Call out commands such as 'Walk forward', 'Stop and turn around', 'Walk down the slope', 'Cross over the footpath', 'Climb up the steps', 'Walk around the sandpit', 'Walk across the stepping stones' and 'Crawl under the slide'.

Key vocabulary: Walk, travel, crawl, climb, slide, over, under, down, up, across, through, around, turn, forward, backward, stop, start.

Extension ideas: Invite volunteers to take over the lead and call out directional instructions.

Practise giving and following directional commands.

Use sports games to learn about direction and position.

Activity 4: Crazy Croquet

Type of activity: Adult-initiated, during independent play.

Resources: Grassy area, croquet mallets or plastic hockey sticks, wire hoops, rubber balls, cones, large wooden blocks to make ramps, big cardboard postal tubes to make tunnels.

What to do: Set up an alternative to crazy golf. Space out some wire hoops evenly and add in some ramps and tunnels. Place some cones around and about so they are in the way. Provide the children with croquet mallets or plastic hockey sticks.

Invite the children to come and play. Explain they must direct their balls so they travel around the cones, through the hoops and tunnels and over the ramps. Join in and model the use of directional language as you play.

Key vocabulary: Direct, control, around, move, over, under, through.

Extension ideas: Ask the children if they have any ideas for how they can make the course more interesting.

Activity 5: Jelly beans

Type of activity: Adult-led, groups of eight.

Resources: Large parachute.

What to do: Divide the children into pairs. Assign a type of bean to each pair. For example, jelly beans (shake like jelly), jumping beans (jump), baked beans (crouch and crawl), runner beans (run). Ask the children to spread out and demonstrate for them how each type of bean moves. Then spend some time calling out the different types of bean so the children can practise how their particular bean moves.

Lay the parachute out on the floor and arrange the children so they are standing around it. Ensure each child is standing on the opposite side to their partner, so the children in each pair are facing one another. Explain that when you call out a type of bean the two children from the appropriate pair must move under the parachute in the style of their bean to swap places with their partner, while avoiding crashing into each other.

Key vocabulary: Move, avoid, under, shake, jump, run, crouch, crawl.

Extension ideas: Change the types of bean around so each pair has a chance to move in different ways.

Activity 6: Busy Bee

Type of activity: Adult-initiated, during independent play.

Resources: Bee-bot® or similar programmable toy, building blocks.

What to do: Challenge the children to arrange some building blocks to make a maze. Explain they are going to send Bee-bot through the maze so the pathways need to be wide enough for him to drive along and turn around. Help the children create their maze and talk about where the bricks are being placed in relation to each other.

When the maze is complete allow the children to program Bee-bot and send him through it. Help them think about what direction he needs to move in to reach a particular place. Listen to their conversation as they play and make comments, modelling the use of directional language.

Key vocabulary: Forward, backward, around, left, right, turn, route, path, stop, start, begin, dead end.

Extension ideas: Invite the children to alter the maze and add features such as bridges and tunnels for Bee-bot to travel over, under and through.

Enhancing continuous provision

Children will naturally explore space and movement during independent play. However, practitioners can provide resources that will prompt children to think more carefully about coordinating their movements and negotiating space.

As well as using flowerbeds, sand and water trays as settings for small world scenarios that involve moving and manipulating characters and animals, make the most of large outdoor spaces by setting up obstacle courses and roadways. Challenge the children to invent games that involve moving and dodging or tracking and searching. Provide mark-making utensils for them to make their own maps and mazes and set up role-play situations that make good use of space. All the time engage the children in conversation about what they are doing and where they are going.

Area of provision	Enhancements that help children develop a sense of space
Water	Turn the water tray into an aquarium. Line the bottom with gravel and add tunnels, plastic plants and ornaments. Provide toy boats and fish for the children to move around and through the obstacles.
Sand	Turn the sand tray into a pirate treasure island. Bury miniature treasure chests and place small palm trees and rocks around and about. Dampen the sand so you can draw arrows and pathways in it. Provide toy pirate figures for the children to direct to the treasure.
Construction	Provide boxes, blocks, planks and guttering for children to make motocross courses for small racing cars. Provide laminated aerial photos of roadways for the children to use as inspiration.
Role Play	Delivery company: Set up an office with table, clipboard, pens and phone, provide numbered cars, mobile phones and packages for delivery. Tour bus: Set out chairs, provide a steering wheel, clipboard, pen, mobile phone, tickets, pretend cameras and microphone. Provide playground chalk for the children to draw roads.
Investigation	Fill a tray with compost, mark out a design and carefully sow cress so that it grows to form a mini maze. Provide toy characters for children to move through it. Use playground chalk to draw a large maze on the floor and write a challenge on the floor that reads, Can you draw a maze of your own?
Physical	Provide bikes and cars for children to practise manoeuvring and negotiating space. Provide large balls for children to dribble, kick and chase. Set out cones for children to weave in and out of on foot and in vehicles.
Garden	Set up a miniature treasure hunt. Hide gold coins in and around the shrubbery and plants. Display a chalk board that reads Hunt the treasure. Talk to the children and ask them to describe where they found the coins.

Curriculum links

Learning about space covers the following areas of learning and development:

EYFS	Uses positional language; can describe their relative position such as 'behind' or 'next to'; uses everyday language to talk about position and to solve problems.
NIC	Explores body space through different types of movement; explores movement through space during outdoor activities; understands and uses a range of positional words; explores movement using programmable devices; follows/gives directions from/to a partner for simple movements.
SCE	In movement, games, and using technology can use simple directions and describe positions; can describe, follow and record routes and journeys using signs and words associated with direction and turning.
WFPF	Develops an awareness of position and movement during their own physical activities; follows instructions and gives directions for simple movements; recognises translations and rotations as movements, and combines them in simple ways; begins to understand angle as a measure of turn, and recognises whole, half and quarter turns.

Length

Length is all about how high, tall, wide, deep or long something is. Measuring length is something that children will encounter throughout their lives, for example, when they try on trousers, hang wallpaper or work out how long it will take to reach a destination.

Knowledge of length is underpinned by the following skills and concepts:

- Having an awareness of size

- Being able to use non-standard units such as strides or pencils to measure

- Being able to count accurately

- Understanding and being able to use language such as 'long', 'short', 'tall', 'high', 'deep', 'narrow' and 'wide'

- Understanding that two identical pieces of string lying next to each other are the same length even if one is not completely stretched out and appears shorter

- Understanding that to accurately compare the length of two objects by sight they must be next to each other and in alignment

- Knowing that length is measured in centimetres and in metres

- Being able to read a numbered scale.

Children learn about length through play and practical activities that require them to physically compare and measure objects. When children are outside they can measure on a small and grand scale.

Activity 1: Good throw!

Type of activity: Adult-initiated, during independent play.

Resources: Playground chalk, metre stick, tub of small balls.

What to do: Use playground chalk to draw a set of parallel lines 50cm apart to a distance of about five metres. Invite one child at a time to throw a ball as far as they can. Write the child's name where the ball first bounces. Repeat until all the children have had a turn.

Bring the children together and look at where the balls landed. Find out who threw their balls the furthest and shortest distances. Use the measurements marked out on the floor to tell each child how far they managed to throw their ball.

Key vocabulary: How far? distance, measure, metre, centimetre, furthest, closest, shortest, longest.

Extension ideas: Challenge the children to try different ways of throwing the balls and make them go further.

Find out how far you can throw.

Activity 2: Three Bears' house

Type of activity: Adult-initiated, during independent play.

Resources: Playhouse, table, each of the following in three different sizes – chairs, bowls, spoons, beds and blankets, mummy, daddy and baby teddy bears.

What to do: Turn the playhouse into the house of the Three Bears. Put a table in, lay it with three different sized bowls and spoons and put three chairs around it. Set up three beds; obviously this will depend on space so use three different sized pillows and blankets to made compact beds to fit in a tighter space. Finally sit three different sized bears around the table.

Join in the children's play and talk about the different sized bears and equipment. Encourage the children to match up the bowls, chairs and beds to the appropriate bears.

Key vocabulary: Big, small, medium, biggest, smallest, middle-sized, large, largest, compare, match, order.

Extension ideas: Provide a Goldilocks costume for the children to act out the story.

Activity 3: Hook a duck

Type of activity: Adult-initiated, during independent play.

Resources: Plastic ducks with hooks on their heads, different length bamboo rods with hooks screwed into the ends, coloured electrician's tape, playground chalks.

What to do: Wrap some coloured tape around the end of each rod (this is to indicate where the rod should be held). Use playground chalk to draw a straight line on the floor. Place the different length bamboo rods on the line so they are pointing out straight ahead. Place a duck at the tip of each rod and draw a circle around each (for future reference). Leave the ducks where they are and pick up the rods and put them in a pile.

Challenge the children to come and hook a duck. Explain they must use the rods but stand on the line and not move closer to the ducks. They must also keep their hands on the taped part of the rod. This means they need to choose the right length rod to reach each duck.

Key vocabulary: Length, long, short, longer, shorter, reach.

Extension ideas: Ask the children to say by sight which ducks are the closest and furthest away. Use a measuring tape to measure the actual distance of each duck from the line.

HOME LINKS

Send home a challenge to find out who is the tallest member of the family. Ask parents to help their children measure the height of each member in their household, write down the measurements and help their children work out who is tallest.

Use string to measure tricky lengths.

Activity 4: How long is a piece of string?

Type of activity: Adult-led, small groups.

Resources: Large roll of paper, toy vehicles, shallow containers, different coloured poster paints, different coloured wool, scissors, tape measure.

What to do: Roll out a large piece of paper on the floor and invite children to dip the wheels of toy vehicles in paint and roll them on the paper to make long wavy tracks. Get them to choose different colours so each can be identified and followed easily.

Give out some tape measures and ask the children to measure their tracks. Help them attempt to bend their tape measures around the wavy tracks. Try a couple of times then ask the children why it is not working. Suggest you try again but this time use string. Help each child lay the string along their track. Cut the string, lift it and stretch it out against the tape measure to find the actual length.

Key vocabulary: Measure, length, longest, shortest, compare, how long? next to, centimetres.

Extension ideas: Ask the children to order the pieces of wool from shortest to longest. Use chalk to write the actual measurements in centimetres next to each length.

Activity 5: Sticks in a line

Type of activity: Adult-led, small groups.

Resources: Bamboo sticks (all the same length), small whiteboard, whiteboard marker.

What to do: Begin by showing the children the bamboo sticks. Talk about taking care not to wave them around and to look before lifting them so as not to poke anyone in the eye.

Point to a landmark, for example a climbing frame or large planter. Explain you would like the children to find out how many sticks laid end-to-end would be needed to reach the target. Before they start, ask them to guess how many sticks think they might need and write their suggestions on a whiteboard.

Let the children work together and line the sticks up along the ground to reach the target. If need be help them to consider the straightest path in light of any obstacles that may be in the way. When they have finished ask them to count the sticks and compare the actual number with their earlier guesses.

Key vocabulary: How many? how far? distance, measure, straight.

Extension ideas: Invite other groups to come and repeat the activity but aiming for different targets. Then bring everyone together to compare the distances and work out which are the shortest and longest. Can the children tell just by looking which objects are the closest and furthest from where they are standing?

Ask the children to suggest different ways to measure distance, by counting paces, for example.

Begin with using non-standard measures.

Don't forget to think about...

...young children should use informal measures to gain a basic understanding of length. This may include using paces or strides, rope, sticks or unifix cubes. There is no harm in providing tape measures and rulers for children to play with, however, as it is also a good idea to model the use of such equipment.

Enhancing continuous provision

Like all aspects of mathematics children's understanding of length is synonymous with their acquisition of the related language. It is therefore important that practitioners observe and join play to model the correct use of vocabulary associated with measuring and comparing length.

Provide resources that will encourage the children to experiment with measuring length. Ensure these include

a mix of non-standard measuring tools, as well as standard equipment with numbered scales. Add features to the environment that will stir their curiosity, for example, paint a height chart on an outside wall, draw a measuring scale on the floor with playground chalk or dip hands in paint to create a numbered hand-print scale up the side of a fence post.

Area of provision	Enhancements that help children develop an understanding of length
Water	Provide different lengths of guttering and piping for children to arrange, match, compare and link together. Set a challenge to: Make the longest waterway you can.
Sand	Provide match and measure dinosaur bones and different length twigs and sticks. Set a challenges such as: Find out how deep the sand pit is and Who can dig the longest trench?
Construction	Provide tape measures, rulers and trundle wheels, as well as playground chalk for marking out measurements and clipboards, paper and pencils for making notes. Provide bricks, blocks and cardboard boxes for building towers.
Role Play	Set up a washing line and provide pegs and a washing basket containing different length scarves, socks, ties and skirts. Set challenges such as: Hang the socks in order from shortest to longest.
Investigation	Provide lengths of ribbon, string, rope, laces, chain, doweling rod, unifix cubes, links, lolly sticks and strips of paper for children to measure with. Provide tape measures and flexible plastic number lines and set a challenge to: Find out which is taller; the climbing frame or the slide?
Physical	Provide climbing frames and climbing walls for children to explore height. Make some example paper planes and provide paper for the children to make their own and test how far they will fly.
Garden	Place different length toy worms and snakes in and around the shrubbery for children to discover and compare. Provide gardening tools, pots, compost, sunflower seeds and beans for children to plant and observe their growth.

Curriculum links

Learning about length covers the following areas of learning and development:

EYFS	Orders two or three items by length or height; uses everyday language to talk about size and distance and to solve problems.
NIC	Compares and orders up to three objects of different length; understands and uses the language of comparison; finds an object of similar length; begins to explore the notion of conservation of length in practical situations; chooses and uses, with guidance, non-standard units to measure length.
SCE	Experiments with everyday items as units of measure to investigate and compare sizes in the environment, sharing findings with others.
WFPF	Compares and orders two or more objects in terms of length/height by direct observation; uses uniform non-standard units for comparison, and sees the need for standard units of measure; uses standard metric units of length; chooses units and measuring equipment appropriate to a relevant measuring task; reads a scale with some accuracy.

Weight

Weight is all about how heavy something is. Children learn about weight through first-hand experience of lifting, moving and handling. They hold objects in their hands and physically weigh them up, and fill bucket scales, watching the balance tip as they add and take away from each side.

Children need to know how to measure weight for many reasons, such as being able to bake, buy pick 'n' mix at the cinema and pack according to an airliner's baggage allowance.

Knowledge of weight is underpinned by the following skills and concepts:

- Being able to use non-standard units such as pebbles or bricks to measure

- Being able to count accurately

- Understanding and being able to use language such as 'light' and 'heavy'

- Understanding that weight is not related to size

- Knowing that weight is measured in grams and kilograms

- Being able to use standard accurate measuring weights and read a numbered scale.

When outside, children have room to explore weight in relation to size. They also have access to large equipment, allowing them to experiment with moving heavy objects using pulley systems and transportation. The following activities make the most of outdoor space by encouraging children to weigh things up for themselves.

Activity 1: Unruly skittles

Type of activity: Adult-initiated, during independent play.

Resources: Light hollow plastic skittles, heavy wooden skittles, large tub.

What to do: Set up some light hollow plastic skittles in an open spot on a slightly breezy day. Put some heavier wooden skittles in a tub nearby. Invite some children to come and play. Each time the skittles blow over complain and ask the children if they know why.

Mention the breeze and ask the children if they have any ideas about how to solve the problem. Try playing the game with the heavier wooden skittles. Can the children explain why it is working better? Talk about the different materials and encourage them to compare the weights by holding one type of skittle in each hand. Explain the weight of the wooden skittle is weighing it down helping to keep it standing, whereas the lighter plastic skittles are blown over much more easily.

Key vocabulary: Lighter, heavier, compare, weight.

Extension ideas: Do this activity with empty plastic bottles and ask the children if they have an ideas about how to make heavier.

Big does not always mean heavy.

Activity 3: Uphill struggle

Type of activity: Adult-initiated, during independent play.

Resources: Bee-bot and trailer, marbles, small wooden bricks, real coins, plastic counters, conkers, sycamore seeds, feathers, leaves, pebbles, stones, ramp.

What to do: Set up a ramp and hook up Bee-bot with a trailer. Provide a variety of objects for the children to load into Bee-bot's trailer and carry up the ramp.

Talk about the different objects and ask the children to tell you which are heavier and lighter. Can they guess which items will be easier for Bee-bot to carry to the top?

Test out different loads and watch to see which Bee-bot struggles with. Help the children consider how to make the journey easier for Bee-bot when he is carrying a heavy load, for instance, reducing the load by removing some objects.

Key vocabulary: Heavy, light, full, less, more, heavier, lighter, compare, easier, harder.

Extension ideas: Provide bucket scales to compare the weights of different loads.

Activity 2: Appearances can be deceiving

Type of activity: Adult-initiated, during independent play.

Resources: Giant balloons, giant cuddly toys, large and small cardboard boxes, shredded paper, dried beans, toys, parcel tape, tennis, cricket, golf and table tennis balls.

What to do: Set out a range of different sized objects in the outdoor area. Put out very large lightweight objects like a giant cuddly toys and inflatables. Fill a small box with dried beans and seal it. Fill a very large box with shredded paper and seal it. Put out a section of toys that vary in weight and size. Blow up some different sized beach balls and fill a tub with tennis, cricket, table tennis and golf balls.

Invite children over, ask them to look at the objects and guess which are the heaviest/lightest. Allow them to pick up the objects to find out if they guessed correctly. Talk about and compare size and weights.

Key vocabulary: Heaviest, lightest, biggest, smallest, heavier, lighter, compare, weigh, feel, guess.

Extension ideas: Help the children arrange the objects in a line from lightest to heaviest.

Provide wheelbarrows and trolleys for children to transport heavy loads.

Activity 4: Heavy load

Type of activity: Adult-initiated, during independent play.

Resources: Large rocks, stones and pebbles, small wheelbarrows, small buckets.

What to do: Fill some buckets with large stones and place a couple of wheelbarrows nearby. Invite some children over and explain you need help moving the stones but have realised they are very heavy to carry. Invite the children to try and lift the buckets. (Make sure they bend their knees to protect their backs.) Ask them if they have any ideas about how to move the stones without having to lift them.

Key vocabulary: Heavy, lift, move, easier, harder.

Extension ideas: Ask the children to fill the buckets with other materials to see if they are easier/harder to move.

Activity 5: Feeling heavy

Type of activity: Adult-led, whole group.

Resources: Large open space, feather, big bouncy ball, wooden brick, large leaf, 50 pence coin.

What to do: Ask the children to form a very large circle. Stand in the middle, pick out an object, hold it up in the air and drop it. Watch it descend and land then ask the children if they can describe how it fell. Could they tell from watching how the object moved whether it was heavy or light? Repeat with the other objects.

Ask the children to spread out and find a space. Explain you are going to call out the name of an object and you would like them to think about if it is heavy or light and move like it would if thrown in the air.

Key vocabulary: Heavy, light, float, drop, fall, bounce, spring, flutter, drift.

Extension ideas: Ask the children to look around and find other objects to test. Before dropping each object, ask them to guess what they think is going to happen.

HOME LINKS

Paste photos of everyday objects that can be found at home, for example a mug, cuddly toy, book and DVD on a worksheet. Ask parents to help their children weigh up the items in their hands, compare them and decide which is the heaviest/lightest. Suggest they check their answers using kitchen scales.

Activity 6: Market day

Type of activity: Adult-initiated, during independent play.

Resources: Tables, baskets, bucket scales, multi-weight scales, till, toy money, paper bags, lolly sticks, small pieces of card, pens, sellotape, scissors, real fruit and vegetables, paper bags.

What to do: Invite the children to help you set up a fruit and veg market in the outdoor area. Help them open up packs of fruit and vegetables, load them into baskets and set them out on tables. Place different types of weighing scales along the stall holders' side. Help the children make price labels; write a price per kilo for each item on pieces of card, tape them to lolly sticks and stand them in amongst the fruit and veg.

Join the children's play and model ordering by weight, for example, 'Please can I have 100g of sprouts and 200g of potatoes?' Help the stall holders use scales to weigh the food and read the scales. Model ordering the items by amount, for example, 'Please can I have a bag of grapes and the same weight in oranges?' Then help the stall holders use bucket scales to find out how many oranges weighs the equivalent of a bag of grapes.

Key vocabulary: Weigh, weight, heavy, heavier, light, lighter, same, balance, compare, grams, kilograms.

Extension ideas: Provide pebbles or gram and kilo weights for children to use with balance scales.

Enhancing continuous provision

When outside there is a lot of scope for children to explore and examine the weights of different objects and materials. Provide a variety of different sized containers for children to fill and move, as well as wheelbarrows and trolleys to move large and heavy loads. Playing with objects of different sizes made out of different materials will help children to begin to understand that weight is dependent upon what something is made of rather than its size.

The children will probably have access to a small set of balance scales in the indoor maths area. However, there are larger versions on the market and it is a great idea to get hold of a set of big bucket scales to use outside. This apparatus provides scope for handling larger and heavier objects, making weighing a more physical experience.

It is also a good idea to provide standard measuring weights and weighing apparatus with numbered scales for children to gain experience of using and reading accurate measures.

Area of provision	Enhancements that help children develop an understanding of weight
Water	Provide sponges for children to compare the dry and wet weight. Provide plastic and foam shapes for children to see which float and sink. Provide metal boats and plastic boats for children test on the water.
Sand	Bury metal coins, plastic coins, glass gems, plastic jewels and costume jewellery and provide weighing scales for children to weigh and compare their finds. Provide bucket scales and wet and dry sand for children to weigh and compare.
Construction	Provide real, wooden, hollow and plastic bricks for children to handle and compare. Provide giant balance scales for comparing weights.
Role Play	Turn the playhouse into a veterinary clinic: Provide animal carriers, vet uniforms, medical kit, kitchen and bathroom scales for animals, dry cat/dog food, scoops, bucket scales and digital scales for food, feeding bowls, notepads and pens.
Investigation	Provide a tub full of random objects and some bucket scales for children to weigh and compare. Set up a pulley system with a rope and bucket for children to lift heavy objects.
Physical	Provide weighted hula hoops, balls of different sizes and weights, skipping ropes made of rope and plastic cord, plastic and wooden skittles for children to handle and compare.
Garden	Provide wheelbarrows for children to transport loads of soil, sand and gravel. Provide gardening tools made of different materials for children to experience handling wood, metal and plastic and unconsciously develop an awareness of the variations in weight.

Curriculum links

Learning about weight covers the following areas of learning and development:

EYFS	Orders two items by weight; uses everyday language to talk about weight and to solve problems.
NIC	Compares up to three objects of different weight; understands and uses the language of comparison; finds an object of similar weight; begins to explore the notion of conservation of weight in practical situations; chooses and uses, with guidance, non-standard units to measure weight.
SCE	Experiments with everyday items as units of measure to investigate and compare sizes and amounts in the environment, sharing findings with others.
WFPF	Compares and orders two or more objects in terms of mass by direct observation; uses uniform non-standard units for comparison, and sees the need for standard units of measure; uses standard metric units of mass; chooses units and measuring equipment appropriate to a relevant measuring task; reads a scale with some accuracy.

Capacity and volume

Children learn about capacity and volume by filling and emptying a range of containers. They need plenty of experience pouring substances from one container into another and finding out what happens when the containers differ in size and shape. They also need experience of loading and packing solid objects. In everyday life, children will experience measuring capacity and volume when they pour out drinks, water the garden and pack shopping into bags.

Knowledge of capacity and volume is underpinned by the following skills and concepts:

- Being able to use non-standard units such as drops, spoons and cups to measure

- Understanding and being able to use language such as 'full' and 'empty'

- Being able to count accurately

- Understanding that an amount of liquid poured from a stout wide container remains the same when transferred into a tall thin container

- Understanding that solid objects can be arranged in such a way as to take up less space

- Knowing that capacity is measured in litres and pints

- Knowing that volume is measured in cubic centimetres

- Being able to read a numbered scale.

The outdoors is ideal for playing with capacity and volume because children can make a mess and get water on the floor.

Activity 1: Paddington's marmalade factory

Type of activity: Adult-initiated, during independent play.

Resources: Paddington Bear, large deep tray, table, mashers, spoons, funnels, orange jelly, shredded orange peel, plastic jars, easel, whiteboard maker/chalk.

What to do: Fill a large tray with orange jelly and shredded orange peel. Lay out a table with plastic jars, funnels and cooking utensils. Put Paddington Bear nearby next to an easel displaying marmalade orders. Use a simple format, for example, a picture of a full jar with a number next to it. Include orders for half jars, quarter and three-quarter filled jars. Invite some children over and tell them it is Paddington's marmalade factory. Explain he would really like some help filling the jars and getting them ready for delivery.

Key vocabulary: Fill, full, half full, nearly full, empty, a little, a lot, too full, level, container, big, small, funnel.

Extension ideas: Encourage children to count how many spoons of marmalade fit into a jar. Vary the measurements by providing different sized spoons and jars.

Find out how much water different containers will hold.

Activity 2: Have a guess

Type of activity: Adult-led, small groups.

Resources: Water, food colouring, bucket, clear containers in various shapes and sizes.

What to do: Fill a bucket with water. Ask a child to choose a container, dip it in the bucket and fill it to the top. Hold the container up and tell the children it is full. Invite another child to choose another container. Ask the children what they think will happen if you pour the water from the first container into the second. Does the second container look bigger or smaller than the first? Does that mean it will hold more or less water? Tell the child to pour the water from the first container into the second. Can the children use mathematical language to explain why the water overflowed or failed to fill the second container? Repeat the activity with different containers.

Key vocabulary: Pour, fill, empty, overflow, more, less, amount, container, bigger, smaller.

Extension ideas: Introduce containers that have the same capacity but are different in shape.

Activity 3: Full to bursting

Type of activity: Adult-led, small groups.

Resources: Balloons, access to a water tap, waterproof coveralls, large target painted on the wall or floor.

What to do: Bring the children to an outside tap and explain that you are going to fill some balloons and throw them at the target. Fill the first balloon slowly, taking care not to overfill and burst it. While filling the rest of the balloons, make deliberate mistakes. For example, overfill some so water squirts out, and under fill others. Throughout, ask the children if they can explain what is happening; Why did the balloon burst? Why did the water squirt out? Allow the children to throw the balloons at the target. Can the children explain why some balloons burst on impact and others do not?

Key vocabulary: Fill, full, empty, overflow, too much, not enough, a lot, too little.

Extension ideas: Fill the balloons using a funnel and jug instead so the children can see how much water is being poured in and how much each balloon can hold.

HOME LINKS

Advise parents to set up a water tray outside along with plastic bottles, jugs and watering cans.

Help Santa fill and empty his sleigh.

Activity 5: Bubble, bubble, toil and trouble

Type of activity: Adult-initiated, during independent play.

Resources: Cauldrons, Halloween beakers and jugs, toy wands (find these in supermarkets around Halloween time), table spoons, teaspoons, wooden spoons, ladles, pipettes, measuring spoons, whisks, access to water and natural objects, plastic snakes, spiders and bugs, soap flakes, food colourings, table, witch and wizard costumes.

What to do: Make up some pictorial spell recipe cards that encourage children to measure out ingredients. For each recipe, put a picture of each ingredient, for example, coloured water, slime, runny mud or sand. Then next to the ingredient put a corresponding measure using pictures of cups, spoons, jugs, ladles or drops from pipettes. For individual ingredients put pictures of the number of objects, for example, three pictures of spiders.

Set out the above equipment on a table with the recipe cards. Join in and model the use of measuring equipment.

Key vocabulary: Measure, how many? full, empty, count, pour, add, cupful, spoonful, drop, level.

Extension ideas: Add recipes that include half measures. Ask the children to make up their own recipes for spells.

Don't forget to think about...

...your use of language when talking about capacity and volume. Take care not to confuse the two; capacity is how much a container can hold, whereas volume is how much space something takes up.

Activity 4: Santa's sleigh

Type of activity: Adult-initiated, during independent play.

Resources: Large cardboard box, Christmas wrapping paper, old Christmas cards, glue, sellotape, scissors, toys, pillow case or sack, Santa and elf costumes.

What to do: Make a sleigh out of a large cardboard box. Cut the box to shape and cover the outside with Christmas wrapping paper. Ask the children to cut out Christmas pictures from old cards and stick them all over the sleigh to decorate it.

As the children role-play at being Santa and his helpers join in and model the use of mathematical language to talk about filling and emptying the sleigh. Encourage the children to think about how many toys they can fit inside the sack, how many toys they fit in the sleigh, whether there is enough room for Santa to sit in the sleigh and if there is enough room for any passengers.

Encourage the children to look for different sized toys to fill their sacks. Ask them to fill one sack with large toys and another with small. Can they say which sack has the most toys in it? Do they know why they can fit more small toys in a sack than large toys?

Key vocabulary: Fill, load, full, fit, pack, empty, too full, too much, not enough, how many? squeeze, overload.

Extension ideas: Turn the playhouse into a workshop and provide cardboard boxes, wrapping paper and toys for children to select the correct sized boxes for packing and wrapping presents.

Find out how many children will fit inside different sized cardboard boxes.

Enhancing continuous provision

Enhance the outdoor area so that children have free access to a wide range of resources that will develop their understanding of capacity and volume. Provide non-standard measuring equipment, including variously sized containers with objects and materials that can be filled into and transferred between them. Give the children measuring jugs, beakers and syringes so they can also practise reading accurate measuring scales.

Make the water tray interesting by adding slime, food colouring and soap. Fill the sand tray with different materials and substances that can be easily poured. Provide different shaped and sized containers for children to fill and empty and set up challenges that help children to consolidate their understanding of capacity in terms of when something is full, half full or empty.

Area of provision	Enhancements that help children develop an understanding of capacity and volume
Water	Provide different sized and shaped mugs, jugs, bottles, buckets, scaled measuring jugs, cylinders and beakers, pipettes, spoons, ladles and medicine syringes.
Sand	Empty the sand tray and fill it with lentils, rice, beans, flax seed or beads for the children to pour, fill and empty containers. Provide dry sand with different sized buckets, scoops and nesting containers.
Construction	Provide crates, banana boxes, wheelbarrows and trailers for children to fill and pack with bricks. Provide toy dumper trucks with pebbles, stones, shells, pinecones and conkers for the children to fill and empty.
Role Play	Perfumery: Provide small plastic bottles (find miniature toiletry travel bottles in chemists), water, food colouring and essence, funnels, flowers, jugs, measuring spoons and pipettes.
Investigation	Fill a bucket about two thirds full with water and provide some large stones. Display the question, What happens when you drop stones into the bucket? On a rainy day challenge the children to: Find out what happens to puddles when you jump in them.
Physical	Provide balls and different sized baskets. Provide very large cardboard boxes for children to climb inside.
Garden	Provide different sized plant pots and watering cans. Attach a hose to an outdoor tap and provide an attachment to control the flow and pressure of the water.

Curriculum links

Learning about capacity and volume covers the following areas of learning and development:

EYFS	Orders two items by capacity; uses everyday language to talk about capacity and to solve problems.
NIC	Compares up to three objects of different capacity; understands and uses the language of comparison; finds an object of similar capacity; begins to explore the notion of conservation of capacity in practical situations; chooses and uses, with guidance, non-standard units to measure capacity.
SCE	Experiments with everyday items as units of measure to investigate and compare sizes and amounts in the environment, sharing findings with others.
WFPF	Compares and orders two or more objects in terms of capacity and volume by filling or emptying containers; uses uniform non-standard units for comparison, and sees the need for standard units of measure; uses standard metric units of capacity; chooses units and measuring equipment appropriate to a relevant measuring task; reads a scale with some accuracy.

Time

Time is a difficult concept for young children and so it is important in the early years to help them gain a sense of time passing, as well as an awareness of time related change. Children need this basic understanding to help later on when it comes to learning how to tell the time, measure periods of time and calculate time difference.

Knowledge of time is underpinned by the following skills and concepts:

- Being able to count accurately

- Being able to recognise numbers

- Being able to read analogue and digital clocks

- Being able to sequence events

- Understanding and being able to use language such as 'now', 'before', 'after', 'later', 'earlier', 'yesterday', 'today' and 'tomorrow'

- Understanding and being able to use language such as 'fast', 'slow', 'quickest', 'longest' and 'shortest'

- Knowing that time is measured in seconds, minutes, hours, days, weeks, months and years.

Children learn about time through gaining experience of ordering and sequencing events, as well as timing things. Outdoors there is plenty of space for children to explore time through movement.

What's more it is only when outside that they can experience first hand the passing of time through the changing of the seasons.

Activity 1: Birthday display

Type of activity: Adult-led, whole group.

Resources: Display board, digital camera, printer, green, yellow, brown and light blue poster paper, staple gun.

What to do: Link children's birthdays to the seasons by setting up a seasonal birthday display. Print passport sized photos of the children, as well as labels for names, birthdays, months of the year and seasons. Divide the display board into four with seasons using brown, green, yellow and light blue poster paper. Put September, October and November in autumn; December, January and February in winter; March, April and May in spring; and June, July and August in summer. Then add the photos of the children.

On each child's birthday, take a photo of them outside. Print it and add it to the display. As the months go on refer to the display and ask the children what season each birthday was in, what the weather was like and what they were wearing. Point out the dates and talk about how long ago each birthday was in terms of days, weeks and months.

Key vocabulary: Birthday, date, days, weeks, months, season, winter, spring, summer, autumn, weather, change, next, how long ago? how long to go until…? how many days/weeks/months?

Extension ideas: Use the display to work out who are the youngest and oldest in the group. Help the children work out whose birthday is coming up next.

Find out how long it takes to grow a plant.

Activity 2: Jasper's Beanstalk

Type of activity: Adult-initiated, whole group.

Resources: *Jasper's Beanstalk* by Nick Butterworth; sunflower seeds, tomato seeds or beans, compost, plant pots or soil bed, gardening tools, bamboo sticks, string, digital camera.

What to do: Read *Jasper's Beanstalk*. Plant beans, sunflowers or tomato plants with the children and take photos while doing so. Wait for the first shoots to appear and take another photo. Then take further photos each week until the plants are fully grown.

Either display the photos on the inside of windows facing out into the growing area for children to see when outside or create a display inside. As the weeks go on, draw the children's attention to the pictures and talk about how the plants have grown. Point out what they were like a couple of weeks ago compared to now. Ask the children how long they think it will be before the plants are fully grown. Talk about how long it has taken for the plants to grow.

Key vocabulary: Plant, grow, time, change, smallest, shortest, biggest, tallest, getting bigger/taller, last week, a couple of weeks ago, months.

Extension ideas: Laminate the photos and use them for sequencing games.

Activity 3: Wacky races

Type of activity: Adult-led, small groups.

Resources: Radio controlled vehicles, playground chalk.

What to do: Draw a race track on the floor with two wide lanes, a starting line and chequered finishing line. Place two vehicles on the starting line and choose two children to take the controls. Ask the other children in the group which vehicle they think is the fastest and will reach the finish first. Shout, 'Ready, steady go!' to start the race. When it is over bring the children together and talk about what happened. Which was the fastest/slowest vehicle? Which took longest to finish? Which finished in the shortest time?

Key vocabulary: Start, finish, fastest, slowest, quickest, longest, shortest, time.

Extension ideas: Introduce a digital stopwatch and time vehicles as they race down the track.

Find out how many skips you can do in one minute.

Activity 5: Timer challenge

Type of activity: Adult-led, during independent play.

Resources: Sand timer, stop-watch, skipping rope, bouncy balls.

What to do: Invite children to come over and take up a timer challenge. Explain you are going to time the children and find out how many actions they can complete in one minute. They can choose to jump, hop, skip or bounce a ball. Use a stop-watch and invite other children to watch it with you. Use a sand timer as well to demonstrate how time slips away.

Key vocabulary: Time, minute, fast, slow, how many? timer, count.

Extension ideas: Set up an easel and record the children's times. Refer to it later on and talk about who completed the most actions in one minute.

Activity 4: We're going on a bear hunt

Type of activity: Adult-led, small groups.

Resources: *We're going on a bear hunt* by Michael Rosen and Helen Oxenbury, access to grass, soil, water, flowers and plants, small world people, toy bear.

What to do: Share *We're going on a bear hunt* with the children. Explain you would like the children to retell the story using objects and items from around the outdoor area.

Help the children think back to the events in the story. Ask them what the family came across first then go and find some grass. What did they come across next? Send the children to find some water and a container. Find some mud next, then ask the children to suggest what they can use for a forest and snow.

Create a small world scene with the found resources. All the time help the children consider, what came before, after and next in the story. Encourage them to decide how to make a cave, then send them to find a bear to put inside. Then act out the whole story using small world characters.

Key vocabulary: First, next, before, after, last, return, back

Extension ideas: Take photos of the story scenes, print and laminate them for use in sequencing activities.

Provide child-friendly stopwatches for children to use.

Enhancing continuous provision

Simply spending time outside on a daily basis will ensure children experience first-hand the passing of time through the changing of the seasons. However, below are some ideas for how to help children develop a sense of time by setting up play scenarios that feature daily routines, shift working and seasonal activities.

In addition, introduce the concept of measuring time by providing sand and digital timers and setting fun challenges for the children to have a go at. As the children play, join them and model the use of vocabulary associated with standard units of time such as seconds, minutes and hours.

Area of provision	Enhancements that help children develop an understanding of time
Water	Provide bottles with different sized holes in the bottom, jugs and watering cans with different spouts and sprinklers for children to pour and sprinkle water and experience fast and slow flow.
Sand	Provide buckets and spades and display a challenge, How many sandcastles can you make in five minutes?
Construction	Provide sand timers and display a challenge, Who can build the tallest tower before the sand runs out? Display a pictorial 'Day in the life of a builder' on an easel. Include pictures of builders arriving at work, working, taking tea breaks, having lunch, receiving deliveries and going home.
Role Play	Night duty: Set up a role-play emergency service such as accident and emergency, fire or police. Set up sleeping quarters for naps. Use gold paper to stick shiny headlights on role-play vehicles and provide night time resources such as torches and reflective jackets.
Investigation	Provide different time-length sand timers and set challenges such as: How many skips can you do in one minute? Can you stand absolutely still for two minutes? How many times can you drive the car around the track in five minutes? How long does it take to run from the shed to the climbing frame?
Physical	Set up a race track: Provide rubber eggs and spoons, beanbags, bucket stilts and stopwatches for children to race each other and practise timing each other.
Garden	Provide laminated gardeners' calendars for the children to refer to during their play. Make seasonal calendars featuring pictures of fruit, vegetables and plants. Make 'jobs to do' calendars featuring pictures of gardening tasks that should be done at particular times of the year, such as clearing leaves, weeding flower beds or harvesting beans. Provide tools and equipment for the children to get on with the jobs independently.

Curriculum links

Learning about time covers the following areas of learning and development:

EYFS	Anticipates specific time-based events such as mealtimes or home time; orders and sequences familiar events; measures short periods of time in simple ways; uses everyday language to talk about time and to solve problems.
NIC	Sequences up to three familiar events; talks about significant times on the clock; compares two intervals of time, talks about observations in terms of took longer/shorter time; explores time patterns; chooses and uses, with guidance, non-standard units to measure time; talks about their work.
SCE	Are aware of how routines and events in their world link with times and seasons, and have explored ways to record and display these using clocks, calendars and other methods.
WFPF	Recognises the time of day and understands the passage of time in relation to daily activities and life events; knows and orders days of the week, the months and seasons of the year; sequences two or more familiar events; gradually reads the time to the quarter hour on an analogue clock, and relate this to digital time.

Money

Children are surrounded by the language of money from an early age, being privy to parental conversations about shopping budgets and holiday savings and told a toy they want is too expensive. Being able to identify different coins and notes and knowing what value they hold is extremely important for children as future shoppers. However, it is equally essential that children are helped to become financially aware in terms of saving, budgeting and value for money.

Knowledge of money is underpinned by the following skills and concepts:

- Knowing that British money is measured in pence and pounds

- Being able to identify different coins and notes

- Understanding and recognising that different coins and notes have particular values

- Being able to recognise numbers

- Understanding and being able to use language such as 'price', 'cost', 'amount', 'change', 'expensive', 'cheap' and 'how much?'

- Understanding that the first price is not always the best.

In the early years children should become familiar with money and gain some understanding of value. They should have experience of handling real money, differentiating between coins and playing shopping games. **Safety note:** Take care when using small coins with young children and prevent them from putting them in their mouths.

Activity 1: Fairy tales

Type of activity: Adult-led, small groups.

Resources: Small cardboard boxes (After Eight chocolate boxes are good), gold wrapping paper, black permanent marker, real coins, toy fairies, paper and pen.

What to do: Wrap the boxes in gold paper, taking care to ensure the lids can be opened and closed. Use the marker pen to draw on details and make the boxes look like small treasure chests. Fill each chest with a variety of real coins. Hide the chests in the garden area and sit a fairy on top of each. Write a letter from Fairyland explaining that some mischievous fairies have taken the Tooth Fairy's coins and hidden them. They were last sighted in your local area. The fairies must be found and the coins returned before sun down when the Tooth Fairy will be leaving on her rounds. At the bottom of the letter put pictures of 1p, 2p, 5p, 10p, 20p and 50p coins with a number next to each to show the number of coins missing.

Read the letter from Fairyland to the children and send them off in search of the coins. When they find the first chest, get them to open it and sort the coins. Look at how many coins there are compared to what the letter shows are missing. Send the children off to find another chest, sort the coins and look at how many they have now. Continue until all the coins have been found.

Thank the children and tell them you will ensure the tooth fairy gets the coins back before the end of the day.

Repeat the activity for other groups of children on later dates. Pretend the same fairies have been up to mischief again.

Key vocabulary: Coins, sort, 1p, 2p, 5p, 10p, 20p, 50p, £1, match, same, how many? enough, more.

Extension ideas: Add up the coins to find the combined value of each.

Think of imaginative ways to play with money.

Activity 2: Money splat

Type of activity: Adult-initiated, during independent play.

Resources: Large laminated photos of 1p, 2p, 5p, 10p, 20p, 50p and £1 coins, roll of sticky backed plastic, buckets, coloured sponges, real coins, basket.

What to do: Spread large laminated photos of coins on the floor and ask someone to help lay some sticky backed plastic over the top. Place some heavy weights around the edge to hold it down. Fill some buckets with water and drop in some coloured sponges.

Ask children to come and pick coins out of the basket and tell you what they are. Then invite them to pick sponges out of the buckets and throw them at the matching coins on the floor.

Key vocabulary: Coin, pence, 1p, 2p, 5p, 10p, 20p, 50p, £1, match, same.

Extension ideas: Remove the basket of real coins and see if the children can identify the coins you call out instead.

Allow children to play with real coins and authentic fake notes.

HOME LINKS

Advise parents to involve their children when visiting local shops. Suggest they ask their children to help count out the correct amount of money and hand it over at the till.

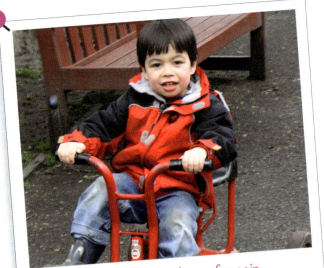

Use outdoor space to make up fun coin recognition games.

Activity 3: Coin exchange

Type of activity: Adult-led, small groups.

Resources: Plenty of 1p, 2p, 5p and 10p coins, two baskets, plenty of small balls, two tubs, vehicle/trike with a storage compartment or trailer, an extra adult.

What to do: Place an adult with a tub of small balls at the far end of an open space. Stand at the opposite end with the children. Choose one child to sit on the vehicle/trike. Explain the child must pedal to the other adult and swap a coin for some balls. Tell them each ball is worth one pence. Invite them to pick a coin out of the basket and say what it is. Help them figure out what the coin is worth before sending them to exchange it for the corresponding number of balls. 1p = one ball, 2p = two balls, 5p = five balls and 10p = ten balls. When the child reaches the far end they must tell the other adult what their coin is and ask for the correct number of balls, return to the start and empty the balls into a tub. Repeat until everyone has had a turn.

Key vocabulary: Coin, pence, 1p, 2p, 5p, 10p, worth, how much? how many?

Extension ideas: Stop using balls and instead have a tub of one pence pieces at the other end.

Activity 4: Shopping trip

Type of activity: Adult-led, whole group, later divided into small groups.

Resources: Paper, pens, real money, shopping bags, enough adults for an off-site trip.

What to do: Bring the whole group together and tell the children you have not got enough food for snack this week. Talk about what you usually eat at snack time and compose a list of items you need. Explain you would like the children's help to go shopping later and buy the food.

Divide the children into smaller groups and write a shopping list for each group. Take the children to a nearby shop and help them to pick and pay for the goods. If possible use a self service check-out give the children experience of scanning, packing and paying for the items independently.

Key vocabulary: Need, shop, buy, list, price, cost, money, pay, till, check-out, how much? total, cheap, expensive, value.

Extension ideas: As you pick the goods from the shelves point out similar products and how they differ in price. Help the children choose less expensive options.

Activity 5: Best value

Type of activity: Adult-initiated, during independent play.

Resources: Tables, tills, purses, handbags, shopping bags, baskets, toy fruit and vegetables, wallets, money belts, real 1p coins, price labels, pens, notepads, old receipts.

What to do: Set up several market stalls. Ensure there are at least two of each type of stall, for example, two fruit and vegetable, two clothing and two bric-a-brac. Price everything between 1p and 10p. The idea is to have expensive and cheap stalls selling the same products. As the children play help them decide which stalls are best value for money. Point out how much the lemons are on one stall compared to the other. Decide which price is higher and therefore which is more expensive. Help them count out the correct amount and look at how much they have left. Talk about how much they can buy with the money they have and how they can make their money go further.

Key vocabulary: Price, more than, less than, more expensive, cheaper, cost, how much? left, pence, compare.

Extension ideas: Mix up the produce so each stall has both cheap and expensive items.

Don't forget to think about…

…the fact that most people now pay for everything using credit and debit cards. This should be reflected in role-play settings so provide tills that include chip and pin devices and display 'cards accepted here' signs on shop doors and garage forecourts.

Enhancing continuous provision

Role-play is the best way to help children develop an understanding of money. The outdoor area provides many practical opportunities for children to play with money and develop an understanding of its worth. Practitioners can set up scenarios that help children learn about working to earn money, saving it and taking care not to waste it. Find role-play suggestions below as well as ideas for games and activities that aim to support coin and note recognition. Provide real coins and authentic pretend notes so children can experience handling the real thing.

Area of provision	Enhancements that help children develop an understanding of money
Water	Drop real coins in water, slime or jelly and provide fishing nets and sorting containers with laminated 1p, 2p, 5p, 10p, 20p, 50p, and £1 labels.
Sand	Bury real coins in the sand and provide metal detectors and sorting containers with laminated 1p, 2p, 5p, 10p, 20p, 50p, and £1 labels. Make sandcastles containing hidden coins.
Construction	Set up a builder's merchant: Fill buckets with gravel and sand, display building blocks, pipes guttering, tools, goggles and hard hats. Put a price on everything and set up a counter with till, notepad and pen. Provide wallets, purses, real coins and pretend notes.
Role Play	Turn the playhouse into a bank: Provide a table, chair, phone, computer keyboard, paper, pens, pencils, chequebooks, money bags and cutlery tray filled with authentic pretend notes and coins. Use a cardboard box to make a cash point and place it just outside. Provide old store loyalty and old membership cards, purses and wallets. Use a banana box to make an armoured vehicle and provide security guard uniforms, lockable cash boxes and fabric money bags. Include a bureau de change counter and provide real examples of foreign currencies for children to play with and compare with British money.
Investigation	Provide a basket full of coins, paper and crayons for children to do coin rubbings.
Physical	Use playground chalk to draw money hopscotch games on the floor; replace numbers with drawings of coins.
Garden	Set up a role-play garden centre: Provide tables, seeds, seed trays, small bags of compost, plant pots, gardening tools, toy lawn mowers, wheelbarrows, buckets and garden ornaments. Put a price on everything and set up a counter with till, notepad and pen. Provide wallets, purses, real coins and pretend notes.

Curriculum links

Learning about money covers the following areas of learning and development:

EYFS	Is beginning to use everyday language to talk about money and to solve problems.
NIC	Uses money in various contexts, talks about things that they want to spend money on, understands the need to pay for goods, becomes familiar with coins in everyday use, talks about different ways we can pay for goods, for example, cash, cheque, credit/debit card, uses their number skills in shopping activities.
SCE	Is developing an awareness of how money is used and can recognise and use a range of coins.
WFPF	Understands and uses money; develops an awareness of the use of money and its value, initially through role play; recognises, sorts and uses coins; finds totals, and gives change.

Planning and organising outdoor mathematics

Every setting has a different outdoor environment with particular features and limitations. A large area needs to be designed carefully to ensure the best possible use of space. On the other hand, practitioners with small outdoor areas need to think about how they can make use of nearby public spaces or the possibility of taking regular trips further afield.

When planning and organising outdoor mathematical provision it is important to think about how the outside environment can be utilised to complement and extend the learning that is happening indoors. Outdoor provision is about taking advantage of the unique characteristics of the outside environment and using them to enhance teaching and learning. Plan physical activities that get children playing with mathematical concepts and actively using mathematical knowledge to develop skills.

Plan outdoor learning in the same detail as you would the indoor space. Draw a diagram of both the indoor and outdoor areas including permanent fixtures. Photocopy these and use one for each day of the week. Handwrite planned activities and resources onto the diagrams, ensuring you consider logistics in terms of indoor and outdoor supervision. Take account of where adult-led activities are to be carried out during each session and plan so that adults are occupying both spaces at all times.

If possible, make life easier by setting up early in the morning before the children arrive. Otherwise pass the planning diagram to a support assistant and ask them to set up while the children settle in during the first fifteen minutes of the day.

Maths in a large outside space

Practitioners who are lucky enough to have a large space should consider providing the following:

- Resources for physical maths games, including skittles, balls, skipping ropes, quoits, cones and giant dice

- Big construction equipment for children to build on a large scale

- A sheltered role-play area that can be used to set up scenarios that promote the use of mathematical language

- Chalkboards, easels and playground chalks for children to record mathematical thinking

- Large sand and water play equipment, such as buckets, pipes, guttering and wheelbarrows for children to experiment with measures on a large and messy scale

- A climbing frame for children to physically explore shape and space

- Number snakes, number squares, targets and hopscotch games painted on walls and floors.

Maths in a small outside space

Practitioners who have a smaller space might like to consider providing the following:

- Functional dividers such as large storage containers or planters to make the best possible use of space while sectioning off areas

- Numbers painted on fencing panels and posts

- Number snakes, number squares an height charts painted on walls

- Wheeled trolleys with stacked baskets or easily movable storage boxes for transporting resources between indoor and outside areas

Think about how the outside environment can be utilised to complement and extend the learning that is happening indoors.

- Number and shape mobiles hanging from trees or shelters

- Pop-up tents for role-play settings

- Sand and water trays to explore measures on a smaller yet still messy scale

- Hand held whiteboards, chalkboards and clipboards for children to record mathematical thinking.

No matter what size the outdoor area is the children should have free and open access to a range of resources so they can choose the things they need, helping them to independently sustain and develop their play. What's more, the layout should, as far as possible, be organised so the children have access to a variety of spaces that facilitate physical activity, as well as quiet play and conversation.

Don't forget to think about...

...planning outdoor experiences that complement and extend indoor learning. The resources and activities should capitalise on the unique nature of the outdoor environment. Plan activities that make the most of the space available, use the natural resources around you and remember there is no need to restrict noise.

Collecting evidence of children's learning

The EYFS highlights observation as integral to teaching and learning. It is through observing children that practitioners get a rounded view of their interests, learning needs and attainment levels. The Framework states learning experiences should be shaped according to observation outcomes. Some children do most of their learning outside and it is just as important to observe outdoors as it is indoors.

Observing outdoors

Make observation outdoors as logistically possible as it is indoors. Ensure practitioners have the correct equipment to hand so they can carry out good quality observations when outside:

- Secure wall-mounted slings or wallets just inside the doorway leading out to the outdoor area. Use it to keep clipboards,

pens, post-it notes and cameras that practitioners can reach in and grab quickly when the need arises.

- Print off sheets of sticky labels for snap-shot observations. Design a template for each label with headings including, name of observer, date, time, name of child, area of learning and observation. These are quick to fill in and easy to transfer to assessment profiles.

- Fill waterproof bum bags with pens, post-its and digital cameras.

- Ensure every clipboard has a few plastic sleeves on it to protect notes from rain and messy play.

- Use dictaphones to record children's thoughts and comments as they play. This is more practical during messy physical activities that make holding a clipboard awkward.

Observation should be a fully inclusive process during which practitioners draw information from a variety of sources to gain a rounded view of the child. However, the EYFS acknowledges the burden of too much paperwork and stresses assessment should not be carried out at the expense of interacting with the children.

Bearing this in mind, the example observation sheet on page 80 is designed to hold a large amount of information on a single document. There is space for recording the observation and assessment notes, as well as comments from other professionals, children and parents.

Observing and assessing mathematical learning

When observing mathematical play it is helpful to have a list of assessment questions to refer to. Either attach the list to your clipboard or include them on observation sheets (see the example on page 80) to help keep curriculum requirements in mind while observing. The list should help you to consider whether the children are:

- Able to explain what they are doing

- Using mathematical language

- Devising methods to solve problems

- Drawing on their knowledge of number

- Using calculation strategies

- Engaging in mathematical mark-making.

When observing an adult-led maths activity it is helpful to observe with specific learning objectives in mind. There are different ways to do this. Either ensure the objectives are clearly stated in the planning and copy them onto observation sheets or include an assessment section on planning documents to record observation notes.

Assessing outdoor provision

Assess the use of outdoor space and resources by observing children's movements. This can be done through tracking observations, where practitioners focus on one child at a time and track their movements on a diagram of the outdoor area. The practitioner may either observe a child continuously for 10 minutes or for five minutes every 15 minutes over the course of an hour. They track the child's movements

Ensure practitioners have the correct equipment to hand so taking good quality observations is just as possible outside.

from one activity to the next and record how long the child remains at each. By choosing to observe a good cross section of children in one session practitioners can gain a clear picture of how well the outdoor space is working to suit particular needs and purposes.

Tracking observations can also be used to help practitioners assess how well subject-specific resources are working to enhance learning. This involves observing particular spaces and the use of resources instead of focusing on specific children. In the case of maths, practitioners may choose to observe how often children play with number squares and snakes painted on the floors. It might be that children simply skip over and ignore them, leading practitioners to consider what games or activities they can plan, as well as resources they can provide to make these mathematical features more attractive and useful.

Don't forget to think about...

...using digital observations to capture snapshots of children's learning. Photographs and film recordings save time and capture a much more rounded picture than hurried handwritten notes.

Maths observation record

Maths observation record

Child's name:

Observer's name:

Area of provision/Focused activity:

Specific learning objectives:

Date:

Start time:

End time:

Observation notes:
Record here children's actions, comments and conversation.

Assessment questions:
Consider these questions in relation to the above observation.

Is the child…

Able to explain what s/he is doing?

Devising methods to solve problems?

Using calculation strategies?

Using mathematical language?

Drawing on his/her knowledge of number?

Engaging in mathematical mark-making?

Assessment notes:

Implications for future planning:
Note down here any ideas stemming from this observation about investigations, activities or resources that build upon the findings of this observation.

Resources and further reading

Resources

- Ribbon wands, stilts, bats, balls, giant dice, beanbags, ankle skips, tunnels, pull along trucks, parachutes, gardening tools, trikes (www.eduzone.co.uk)

- High vis vests, strap kits, outdoor clothing, outdoor kitchen, garden workbenches, weather resistant learning boards, chalk boards (www.earlyyearsdirect.com)

- Number pebbles, squidgy sparkly numbers, numicon, large foam shapes (www.earlyyearsresources.co.uk)

- Cork and dowel construction, sinking ships, mud kitchen, market stall, drawing and construction tiles, wide range of outdoor mark-making resources (www.playforce.co.uk)

- Crates, pallets, decking, pipes, guttering and stands, giant balance scales, measuring tapes and sticks, number bunting, metal numbers, timers, rustic numbers, number stepping stones (www.cosydirect.com)

- Number pebbles, match and measure dinosaur bones, multi-weight scales, measuring snakes, dinosaurs, dragons, fairies, minibeasts (www.yellow-door.net)

- Glass pebbles, jelly stones, seashells, acrylic stones, sorting sets and containers, pretend money, tills, outdoor shop, washing line, giant outdoor abacus (www.tts-group.co.uk).

Further reading

- *50 Fantastic Ideas for Maths Outdoors* by Kirstine Beeley (Featherstone, 2013)

- *Foundations of Mathematics* by Carole Skinner and Judith Stevens (Featherstone, 2012)

- *Learning Outdoors in the Early Years* by Carol Bratton, Una Crossey, Dawn Crosby and Wendy McKeown (CCEA, 2005)

- *Maths Outdoors* by Mercia Lee and Helen Yorke (Lawrence Educational, 2007)

- *Maths Outdoors* by Carole Skinner (Nelson Thornes, 2005)

- *Open Up to Outdoor Mathematics* by Gail Ryder Richardson (Learning Through Landscapes, 2007) Accessed online: http://outdoormatters.co.uk/open-up-to-outdoor-mathematics/

- *Outdoor Learning in the Early Years: Management and Innovation* by Helen Bilton (Routledge, 2010)

- *Outdoor Play* by Sue Durant (Practical Pre-School Books, 2013)

- *The Little Book of Maths Outdoors* by Terry Gould (Featherstone, 2013)

- *Young Children Thinking Mathematically: PSRN essential knowledge for Early Years Practitioners* by the Department for Children, Schools and Families (DCSF Publications, 2009).

Useful websites

- Community Playthings: http://www.communityplaythings.co.uk/products/outdoor-play

- Creative Star Learning Company: http://creativestarlearning.co.uk/c/maths-outdoors/

- Education Scotland: http://www.educationscotland.gov.uk/learningteachingandassessment/approaches/outdoorlearning/

- Learning Through Landscapes: http://www.ltl.org.uk/

References

Bilton, H. (2010) *Outdoor Learning in the Early Years: Management and Innovation*. Routledge, Oxon.

Bruner, J. (1966) *Toward a Theory of Instruction*. Harvard University Press, Cambridge, MA.

Council for the Curriculum, Examinations and Assessment (CCEA) (2006) *Northern Ireland Curricular Guidance for Pre-School Education*. CCEA, Belfast.

Council for the Curriculum, Examinations and Assessment (CCEA) (2007) *Northern Ireland Curriculum: Primary*. CCEA, Belfast.

Department for Children, Education, Lifelong Learning and Skills (DCELLS) (2008) *Foundation Phase Framework for Children's Learning for 3 to 7-year-olds in Wales*. DCELLS Publications, Cardiff.

Department for Children, Education, Lifelong Learning and Skills (DCELLS) (2008a) *Foundation Phase Framework: Learning and Teaching Pedagogy*. DCELLS Publications, Cardiff.

Department for Education (DfE) (2014) *Statutory Framework for the Early Years Foundation Stage*. DfE Publications, Nottingham.

Learning and Teaching Scotland (LTS) (2010) *Curriculum for Excellence through Outdoor Learning*. LTS, Glasgow.

Piaget, J. (1952) *The Origins of Intelligence in Children*. International Universities Press, New York.

Siraj-Blatchford, I., Sylva, K., Muttock, S., Gilden, R., Bell, D. (2002) *Researching Effective Pedagogy in the Early Years [REPEY]: Research Report No 356*. HMSO, London.

Siraj-Blatchford, I., Sylva, K., Melhuish, E., Sammons, P., Taggart, B. (2004) *Effective Provision of Pre-school Education [EPPE] Project: Final Report*. DfES, London and Institute of Education, University of London.

Sylva, K., Melhuish, E., Sammons, P., Siraj, I., Taggart, B., with Smees, R., Toth, K., Welcomme, W., Hollingworth, K. (2014) *Effective Pre-school, Primary and Secondary Education [EPPSE 3-16] Project: Research Report*. University of Oxford; Birbeck, University of London; Institute of Education, University of London.

Tickell, C. (2011) *The Tickell Review: The Early Yeas: Foundations for life, health and learning*. HMSO, London.

Vygotsky, L. (1986) *Thought and Language*. MIT Press, Cambridge, MA.